THE TRAVELLER'S GUIDE TO THE ASTRAL PLANE

A complete guide to the theory and practice of astral projection, focusing in particular on little-known Eastern techniques.

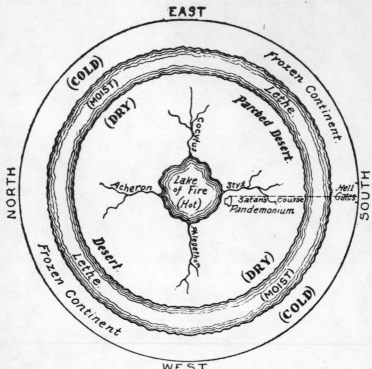

EAST

(COLD)
(MOIST)
(DRY)

Frozen Continent

Lethe

Parched Desert

Cocytus

NORTH

Acheron

Lake
of Fire
(Hot)

Styx

Satan's course

Pandemonium

Hell
Gates

SOUTH

Phlegethon

Desert

Lethe

Frozen Continent

(DRY)
(MOIST)
(COLD)

WEST

FRONTISPIECE

Ancient Greek conception of the world of the dead, from Himes'
Paradise Lost.

THE TRAVELLER'S GUIDE TO THE ASTRAL PLANE

by

STEVE RICHARDS

THE AQUARIAN PRESS

First published 1983

© STEVE RICHARDS 1983

British Library Cataloguing in Publication Data

Richards, Steve
The travellers guide to the astral plane.
1. Astral projection
I. Title
133.9   BF1389.A7

ISBN 0-85030-337-0

The Aquarian Press is part of the Thorsons Publishing Group, Wellingborough, Northamptonshire, NN8 2RQ, England

Printed in Great Britain by
Woolnough Bookbinding Limited, Irthlingborough, Northamptonshire

8   10   12   11   9   7

Contents

1. Suspended Animation

In the mid-seventeenth century a crew of Indian workmen were digging a drainage ditch outside the city of Amritsar, when they suddenly cut into what appeared to be a tomb in the brittle shale. It contained the body of a *sadhu*, which showed no sign of deterioration, in spite of the fact that it had evidently been buried there for some considerable time. The workers disinterred the body and brought it to the surface, 'and in so doing,' says John Keel, 'unwittingly helped launch another one of India's most fascinating mysteries.'[1]

As soon as the sunlight struck the *sadhu's* body, he began to stir. Within a few moments he was completely conscious. He claimed that he had been buried for 100 years, without food, water, or air, and without suffering any ill effects.

He was the the first man to demonstrate the amazing phenomenon known as suspended animation. But he would not be the last. A century and a half later another *sadhu* would appear in the same part of India and make the same claim.

His name was Haridas, and he claimed that he could, with proper preparation, be buried alive, remain underground for any length of time he chose, and be disinterred without experiencing any ill effects. He demonstrated this remarkable skill in the city of Jummu, and later re-peated it at Amritsar, and Jesrota. One of his observers was a government minister named Raja Dhyan Singh, who apparently brought him to the attention of the Maharajah of Lahore, the famous Rundjit Singh. The Maharajah naturally demanded a demonstration, and one was not slow in coming.

For several days prior to his burial, Haridas flushed his bowels in true yogic fashion, and engaged in other activities for bodily purification, including bathing in hot water up to his armpits, and refusing every food except yogurt and milk. Doctors who examined him found that he had cut the tissues under his tongue, so that he could swing his tongue backwards and use it to plug his windpipe. On the day of his burial, he swallowed some thirty yards of linen and regurgitated the whole thing in the presence of several British officers. He then announced that he was ready.

The Maharajah, the French General Ventura, Captain Wade, the British political agent at Lodhiana and the principal Sikh chiefs assembled at a grave of stonework which had been constructed for the occasion. The fakir sealed his ears and nostrils with wax, cast off his clothing, threw back his tongue so that it sealed his gullet, and proceeded to go into a trance. He was then enveloped in a linen bag, which was sealed with the Maharajah's personal seal. The bag was put into a sealed and padlocked chest, and lowered into the grave.

A large quantity of earth was thrown over the chest, and barley was planted on top. Finally, a guard was detailed, comprising four companies of soldiers, with four sentries 'furnished and relieved every two hours, night and day, to guard the building from intrusion'.[2]

With all these precautions, the Maharajah still had doubts, and thrice ordered the fakir to be disinterred. But each time there was Haridas, just as he had been buried, his body cold and lifeless, but mysteriously preserved from decomposition.

At the end of ten months the fakir was disinterred for the last time. General Ventura and Captain Wade raised the chest from the grave, then broke its seals and unlocked its padlocks. 'On opening it,' wrote the Captain, 'the legs and arms of the body were shrivelled and stiff, the face full, the head reclining on the shoulder like that of a corpse. I then called to the medical gentleman who was attending me to come down and inspect the body, which he did, but could discover no pulsation in the heart, the temples, or the arm. There was, however, *a heat about the region of the brain*, which no other part of the body exhibited.'[3] The servants then went about the process of his resuscitation. This

included bathing with hot water, friction, the removal of wax and cotton pledgets from the nostrils and ears, the rubbing of the eyelids with ghee of clarified butter, and, what will appear most curious to many, the application of a hot wheaten cake, about an inch thick, to 'the top of the head'. After the cake had been applied for the third time, the body was violently convulsed, the nostrils became inflated, the respiration ensued, and the limbs assumed a natural fullness. But the pulsation was still barely perceptible. 'The tongue was then anointed with ghee, the eyeballs became dilated and recovered their natural colour, and the fakir recognized those present and spoke.' It should be noticed that not only had the nostrils and ears been plugged, but the tongue had been thrust back so as to close the gullet, thus effectively stopping the orifices against the admission of atmospheric air.[4]

'While in India,' says Madame Blavatsky 'a fakir told us that this was done not only to prevent the action of the air upon the organic tissues, but also to guard against the deposit of germs of decay, which in case of suspended animation would cause decomposition exactly as they do in in any other meat exposed to air.'[5]

Haridas became a favourite of the Maharajah, who gave him enough diamonds and emeralds to make him a man of some means. His feats were studied by several British physicians, including Dr MacGregor, who vouches for the fakir's extraordinary powers in his *Medical Topography of Lodhiana.*[6] 'He might have attained world fame,' wrote Keel, 'except for one sad fact.' He took a strong interest in matters of the flesh. After he deprived several of his lady followers of their highly valued virginity, the government... banished him back to the mountains. He was never heard of again.[7]

Now there is no question about the historical facts here. The same feat has been performed by the famous Egyptian fakir Tahra Bey.

Tahra Bey was born in 1897 to Coptic Christian parents in the city of Tanta – home of the thirteenth-century fakir Sheikh Ayid Ahmad el Badawi. He studied medicine in Constantinople, and for a time maintained a clinic in Greece, but his heart was in the art of the fakirs, an art which he had been studying since childhood.

While in Greece he says he was 'lowered into the very abyss of death' for twenty-eight days and emerged none the worse for his extraordinary experience. Encouraged by this initial success, as well as by the hostility of the Greek Orthodox Church, Tahra Bey abandoned his medical practice and set out to demonstrate his skills in the great world.

After passing through Bulgaria, Serbia, and Italy, he arrived in France, where he was 'buried' for twenty-four hours in a lead coffin filled with sand and completely submerged in water.[8] He claimed that he performed his feats by inducing a state of trance, slowing his heartbeat to a minimum, throwing his head back, retracting his tongue into his throat, and pressing on certain nerve centres in his neck. After he lost consciousness, his assistants would stuff his ears and nose with cotton, thereby rendering it impossible for him to breathe by any surreptitious means.[9]

While in France, he was challenged to a 'duel of the fakirs' by the Frenchmam Paul Heuze. The duel took place in Paris on 11 December 1928 and was joined at the last moment by a French conjurer who called himself 'Karma'. It is notable that M. Heuze was able to reproduce most of Tahra Bey's feats, such as sitting on a bed of nails, but that when he was 'buried alive' he remained immured for only an hour. 'He declared afterwards that there was nothing mysterious about it,' says Rawcliffe, 'and that no state of trance was necessary.'[10] But he had twenty-three hours left to go before he could say that he had done as much as the Egyptian fakir. And even the extraordinary American magician Harry Houdini was able to remain submerged for only an hour and a half under the same conditions.[11]

Yogis who have performed the same feat, however, using trance techniques instead of mere will-power, have repeated Tahra Bey's performances and even surpassed them. On 15 February 1950 the yogi Shri Ramadasji allowed himself to be immured under conditions similar to those of Tahra Bey for an astonishing sixty-two hours! According to Dr Vakil, who supervised the experiment, the *sadhu* was interred in an airtight cement coffin onto which 1400 gallons of water had been pumped. At the conclusion of the experiment he was revived with smelling salts and quickly returned to consciousness, hardly any worse for having undergone such an amazing ordeal.[12]

Western critics who have tried to explain this phenomenon have resorted to several ingenious theories. Rawcliffe suggested that the fakirs use drugs. And John Keel, who showed considerable courage in trying the feat himself, believes that the fakirs merely select a place where the dirt is porous and the air can seep through.[13] But although there is no question that a man can breathe underground this way, that fact in itself does not explain the mystery.

There is an old story in the *Chirurgical Journal* of Leipzig about a fellow who was 'buried alive' in Germany and who had no apparent difficulty breathing for over an hour before losing consciousness. 'The grave was carelessly and loosely filled with an exceedingly porous soil,' says Poe, who relates the tale, 'and thus some air was necessarily admitted', thus vindicating Keel's theory.[14] But this story is a bit different from those of the fakirs and yogis we hear about, because the German was buried by mistake.

He was an artillery officer, who was thrown on his head by an unmanageable horse, and who suffered concussion. Physicians were called, and every remedy known to science at that time was applied, but to no effect, 'Gradually,' says Poe, 'he fell into a more and more hopeless state of stupor, and finally, it was thought that he had died.' What had happened, of course, was that he had fallen into a sleep so profound that all vital signs had ceased. This would appear to be the same kind of trance Haridas and Tahra Bey claimed to be able to induce at will. That fact in itself suggests that such a trance is within the range of human potential. As for the German, his story has an ending of the most ironic sort. Having been rescued from premature burial, the poor fellow fell victim, says Poe 'to the quackeries of medical experiment. The galvanic battery was applied, and he suddenly expired in one of those ecstatic paroxysms which, occasionally, it superinduces.'[15]

There is no question whatever about this phenomonen. Poe himself tells several other stories which are equally interesting. One of these concerns a London lawyer, a Mr Edward Stapleton, who was buried in 1831, without, however, having had the opportunity to die first.

Like the German, and, for that matter, Tahra Bey and Haridas, Mr Stapleton had entered a trance state so profound that he was thought to be dead. He had, after all, suffered from typhus fever, and there was every indication that the disease had claimed his life. His case aroused the curiosity of his physicians, and they decided to continue studying it *post-mortem*, engaging the services of a body snatcher for the purpose. It was the third night after the funeral. 'The supposed corpse was unearthed from a grave eight feet deep,' says Poe, 'and deposited in the operating chamber of one of [London's] private hospitals.'

Mr Stapleton was actually being dissected when one of the surgeons had the idea of using the galvanic battery on him. Imagine the poor doctor's surprise when 'the patient, with a hurried, but quite unconvulsive movement, arose from the table, stepped into the middle of the floor, gazed at him for a few seconds, and then – spoke . . . .. Having spoken, he fell heavily to the floor.'

His words were not understood, but his situation was. He was revived 'upon the exhibition of ether' and 'was rapidly restored to health.' What was most remarkable about this was that whereas Mr Stapleton's *body* was in trance, his *mind* was awake. In fact, according to Poe

he declares that at no period was he altogether insensible – that, dully and confusedly, he was aware of everthing that happened to him, from the moment in which he was pronounced *dead* by his physicians, to that in which he fell swooning to the floor of the hospital. [The words that he spoke, and which no one could understand, were,] I am alive.

This is what makes suspended animation interesting. Haridas told Captain Osborne that while in the state he had the most 'delicious dreams'. He did not elaborate on their nature, but Poe, who had the experience himself, posed a question that seems curiously suggestive in this connection, namely, 'Where, [while the body was in trance], was the soul?'

Now the very act of posing this question seems to imply that it was not with the body itself, since if it was, the answer would be trivial. But Poe must have had dreams of a different sort – if dreams they were – and the same must have been true of Haridas, and the others.

If we believe the yogis, the soul is freed from the body in suspended animation, just as it would be in death itself, the only difference being that in suspended animation it has the option of returning. One could say that it 'projects astrally', to use the commom term, but that would not be completely satisfactory. It ventures forth onto the astral plane, to be sure, but with a critical difference.

Whereas the Western student wishes to project that he may conquer time and space, the Eastern student has a more serious and interesting purpose in mind. He wishes to conquer consciousness itself – to traverse the six realms of *Sangsaric* existence, as the Eastern books say, to visit Heaven and Hell at his pleasure, as well as all the realms between, and eventually to transcend the realms themselves, attaining thereby the state of enlightenment.

In *Focus on the Unknown*, Alfred Gordon Bennett mentions 'a certain writer and occultist' he had known at one time and 'who, after many years' residence in the East', became 'an adept at *Raja Yoga*', and who tried suspended animation himself. He arranged to have himself buried for several days and then disinterred. Bennett writes:

After being revived by prearranged occult means he was able to give a perfectly lucid and rational account of the astral journeys he had undertaken whilst his body lay in *samadhi*.

He spoke of matters – places, people, happenings, and events – which seemed to have no reasonable or rational connection or association with the places, people, happenings, and events likely to be met with or experienced in any of the known normal spatial dimensions. But at the same time, it was patently obvious that he had also travelled extensively *in* our normal dimensions, and the difficulty was, despite the lucidity of his reminiscences, to decide just where this normal travelling ended and his supernormal travelling began.[16]

He says that this difficulty was most pronounced immediately after awakening, and although he gives none of the details of this occultist's experiences, he suggests that such a feat is possible to anyone with sufficient determination and courage.

A more detailed account appeared in the August 1931 edition of *The Rosicrucian Digest* and was signed by Dr James Douglas Ward.

Ward spent some two and a half years studying suspended animation in India, along with three of his countrymen. He says that the methods were quite similar to Western hypnotism, with twelve stages of suggestion and sixty 'intermediate charges'.

In the most advanced stage of trance, the heart shrinks to one half its normal size and the soul takes leave of the body. Astral projection-type experiences are obtained in less advanced stages, he says, but it is not until the most advanced stage is reached that the practitioner is able to project into the higher psychic planes.

He says that the Masters of his school 'called for volunteers to accompany the leading Master out of his body into the spiritual and spend forty-eight hours behind the screen with the veil lifted.' Ward himself volunteered, along with a Hindu and two other Americans named J. M. and J. S. His experiences were extremely mystical.

He says that he 'turned to a plane or condition' where he 'viewed the Celestial Throne, on which was mounted a symbol of the Arc of Safety.' Over that he saw a vision of the Royal Arch of Masonry, which looked with its seven colours like a rainbow in the sky, and through the arch he saw 'woven' the Lost Word. This experience was accompanied by a mystical illumination concerning the Word, which he says he received in the 'sixth degree' of his school, but which had never had the fullness of meaning to him that it did at that moment. He learned why man *had* the Word, and why he thought he had lost it, and yet why it could not *be* lost. He also had certain illuminations concerning the mystical meaning of love, which appear to be more felt than understood.[17]

Another account, which is less mystical, but more detailed, comes from a Dr Wiltse. This is a case of *spontaneous* suspended animation, which came upon him during the summer of 1889, when he was suffering from 'typhoid fever with subnormal temperature and pulse.'

I asked if I was perfectly in possession of my mind, so that what I might say might be worthy of being relied upon. Being answered in the decided affirmative, I bade adieu to family and friends, giving such advice and consolation to each and all as I deemed best, conversed upon the proofs *pro* and *con* of immortality, and called upon each and all to take testimony for themselves by watching the action of my mind, in the bodily state in which they saw me. As my pupils fell open and vision began to fail, and my voice to weaken, feeling a sense of drowsiness come over me, with a strong effort, I straightened my stiffened legs, got my arms over the breast, and clasped the fast stiffening fingers, and soon sank into utter unconsciousness.

I passed about four hours in all without pulse or perceptible heart beat... During a portion of this time several of the bystanders thought I was dead, and such a report being carried outside, the village church bell was tolled. Dr Raynes informs me, however, that by bringing his eyes close to my face, he could perceive an occasional short gasp, so very light as to be barely perceptible, and that he was upon the point, several times, of saying, 'He is dead', when a gasp would occur in time to check him.

He thrust a needle deep into the flesh at different points from the feet to the hips, but got no response. Although I was pulseless about four hours, this state of apparent death lasted only about half an hour.

I lost, I believe, all power of thought or knowledge of existence in absolute unconsciousness. I need not guess at the time so lost, as in such a state a minute or a thousand years would appear the same. I came again into a state of conscious existence and discovered that I was still in the body, but the body and I had no longer any interests in common. I looked in astonishnment and joy for the first time upon myself – the me, the real Ego.

I am about to get out of the body. I watched the process of separation of soul and body. By some power, apparently not my own, the Ego was rocked to and fro, laterally, as a cradle is rocked, by which process its connection with the tissues of the body was broken up. After a little time the lateral motion ceased, and along the soles of the feet beginning at the toes, passing rapidly to the heels, I felt and heard, as it seemed, the snapping of innumerable small cords. When this was accomplished I began slowly to retreat from the feet, toward the head, as a rubbercord shortens. I remember reaching the hips and saying to myself: 'Now, there is no life below the hips.' I can recall no memory of passing through the abdomen and chest, but recollect distinctly when my whole self was collected into the head, when I reflected thus: 'I am all in the head now, and I shall soon be free.' I passed around the brain as if I were hollow, compressing it and its membranes, slightly, on all sides, toward the centre, and peeped out between the sutures of the skull, emerging like the flattened edges of a bag of membranes. I appeared to myself something like a jelly-fish as regards colour and form.

As I emerged, I saw two ladies sitting at my head. There was room for me to stand, but [I] felt considerable embarrassment as I reflected that I was about to emerge naked before them. As I emerged from the the head I floated up and down and laterally like a soap-bubble attached to the bowl of a pipe until at last I broke free from the body and fell lightly to the floor. I slowly rose and expanded into the full stature of a man. I seemed to be translucent, of a bluish cast, and perfectly naked. With a painful sense of embarrassment I fled toward the partially opened door to escape the eyes of the two ladies whom I was facing as well as others who I knew were about me, but upon reaching the door I found myself clothed, and turned and faced the company. As I turned, my left elbow came in contact with the arm of one of two gentlemen, who were standing in the door. To my surprise, his arm passed through mine without apparent resistance. I looked quickly up to see if he had noticed, but he gave me no sign. [He] only stood and gazed toward the couch I had just left. I directed my gaze in the direction of his, and saw my own dead body. I saw a number of persons standing about the body, and particularly noticed two women kneeling by my left side, weeping.

I now attempted to gain the attention of the people with the object of comforting them as well as assuring them of their own immortality. I bowed to them playfully and saluted with my right hand. I passed about among them also, but found that they gave me no heed. Then the situation struck me as humorous, and I laughed outright.

They must certainly have heard that, I thought, but not one lifted their [sic] eyes from my body. It did not occur to me to speak, and I concluded the matter by saying to myself: 'They see only with the eyes of the body. They cannot see spirits. They are watching what they think is I, but they are mistaken. That is not I. This is I, and I am as much alive as ever.'

I turned and passed out the open door. I crossed the porch, descended the steps, and walked down the path and into the street. I never saw that street more distinctly than I saw it then. I took note of the redness of the soil and of the washes the rain had made. I took a rather pathetic look about me, like one who is about to leave his home for a very long time. Then I discovered that I had become larger than I was in earth life, and congratulated myself. I was somewhat smaller in the body than I just liked to be, but in the next life, I thought, I am to be as I desired.

My clothes, I noticed, had accomodated themselves to my increased stature, and I fell to wondering where they came from and how they got on to me so quickly and without my knowledge. I examined the fabric and judged it to be of some kind of Scotch material – a good suit, I thought, but not handsome; still, neat, and good enough. 'How well I feel,' I thought. 'Only a few minutes ago I was horribly sick and distressed. Then came that change, called death, which I have so much dreaded. It is past now, and here am I still a man, alive and thinking, yes, thinking as clearly as ever, and how well I feel. I shall never be sick again. I have no more to die.' In sheer exuberance I danced a figure, and fell again to looking at my form and clothes.

Suddenly I discovered that I was looking at the straight seam down the back of my coat. How is this? I thought. How do I see my back? And I looked again to reassure myself, down the back of the coat, or down the back of my legs to the very heels, I put my hand to my face and felt for my eyes. They are where they should be, I thought. Am I like an owl that I can turn my head half-way round? I tried the experiment and failed.

No! Then it must be that having been out of the body but a few moments, I have the power to use the eyes of my body, and I turned about and looked back in at the open door, where I could see the head of my body in a line with me. I discovered then a small cord, like a spider's web, running from my shoulders back to my body and attaching to it at the base of the neck in front.

I was satisfied that by means of that cord I was using the eyes of my body, and, turning, walked down the street. I had walked but a few steps, when I again lost my consciousness. When I again awoke [I] found myself in the air, where I was upheld by a pair of hands, which I could feel pressing lightly against my sides. The owner of the hands, if they had one, was behind me, and was shoving me through the air, at a swift, but pleasant, rate of speed. By the time I fairly realized the situation I was pitched away and floated easily down a few feet, alighting gently upon the beginning of a narrow, but well-built, roadway, inclining upward at an angle of something less than 45 degrees.

I looked up and could see sky and clouds above me at the usual height I looked down and saw the tops of green trees and thought [that] it [was] as far down to the tree-tops as it is high to the clouds. As

I walked up the road I seemed to face nearly north. I looked over the right side of the road and under it could see the forest, but discovered naught to support the roadway, yet I felt no fear of falling. I examined the material of which it was built. It was built of milky quartz and fine sand. I picked up one of the gravels and looked at it particularly. I remember that it had a dark speck in the centre. I brought it close to my eye and discovered that [the speck] was a small hole apparently caused by chemical action of some metal. There had been a recent rain, and the coolness was refreshing. I noticed that, although the grade was steep, I felt no fatigue in walking, but my feet seemed light, and I rejoiced in my perfect health and strength. As eternal existence was now assured, I had no need to hurry, and so walked very leisurely along, now stopping and looking at the scenery, or looking back at the road, if perchance someone might come along, and occasionally turning and walking backward, and thus watching the road behind me for the company I so strongly desired. I thought certainly someone from the other world would be out to meet me, though, strangely enough, I thought of no person whom above others I desired to see. Angels or fiends, one will come out to meet me – I wonder which it will be? I reflected that I had not believed all the Church tenets, but had written and taught verbally a new, and, I believed, a better, faith. But, I reasoned, I knew nothing, and where there is room for doubt there is room for mistake. I may, therefore, be on my way to a terrible doom. And here occurred a thing hard to describe. At different points around me, I was aware of the expressed thought: 'Fear not, for you are safe!' I heard no voice, I saw no person, yet, I was perfectly aware that at different points, at varying distances from me, someone was thinking that thought for my benefit, but how I was made aware of it was so great a mystery that it staggered my faith in its reality. A great fear and doubt came over me, and I was beginning to be very miserable when a face so full of ineffable love and tenderness appeared to me for an instant as set me to rights upon that score.

Suddenly, I saw at some distance ahead of me three prodigious rocks blocking the road, at which sight I stopped, wondering why so fair a road should be thus blockaded, and while I considered what I was to do, a great and dark cloud, a cubic acre in size, stood over my head. Quickly it became filled with living, moving, bolts of fire, which darted hither and thither. They were not extinguished by contact with the cloud, for I could see them in the cloud as one sees fish in deep water.

The cloud became concave on the upper surface like a great tent, and began slowly to revolve. When it had turned three times I was aware of a presence which I could not see, but which I knew was entering into the cloud from the southern side. The presence did seem to my mind as a form, because it filled the cloud like some vast intelligence. He is not as I, I reasoned. I fill a little space with my form, but He may fill immensity itself at His will, even as He fills the cloud. Then from the right side and the left side of the cloud a tongue of black vapour shot forth and rested lightly upon either side of my head, and as they touched me thoughts not my own entered my brain.

These, I said, are His thoughts and not mine. They may be in Greek or Hebrew for all power I have over them. But how kindly am I addressed in my mother tongue so that I may understand all His will.

Although the language was English, it was so eminently above my power to reproduce that my rendition of it is as far short of the original as any translation of a dead language is weaker than the original. For instance, the expression: 'This is the road to the eternal world' did not contain over four words, neither did any sentence in the whole harangue, and every sentence, had it been written, must have closed with a period, so complete was the sense. The following is as near as I can render it:

'This is the road to the eternal world. Yonder rocks are the boundary between the two worlds and the two lives. Once you pass over them, you can no longer return into the body. If your work was to write the things that have been taught you, waiting for mere chance to publish them, if your work was to talk to private individuals in the privacy of friendship – if this was all, it is done, and you may pass beyond the rocks. If, however, upon consideration you conclude that it shall be to publish as well as to write what you are taught, if it shall be to call together the multitudes to teach them, it is not done, and you can return into the body.'

The thought ceased, and the cloud passed away, moving slowly toward the mountain in the east. I turned and watched it for some time, when suddenly, and without having felt myself moved, I stood close to and in front of the three rocks. I was seized with strong curiosity then to look into the next world.

There were four entrances, one very dark, at the left between the wall of black rock and the left hand one of the three rocks, a low arch-way between the left hand and the middle rock, and a similar one between that and the right hand rock, and a very narrow pathway running around the right hand rock at the edge of the roadway.

I did not examine the opening at the left – I know not why, unless it was because it appeared dark, but I knelt at each of the low archways and looked through. The atmosphere was green, and everything seemed cool and quiet and beautiful. Beyond the rocks the roadway, the valley, and the mountain range curved gently to the left, thus shutting off the view at a short distance. If I were only around there, I thought, I should soon see angels, or devils, or both, and, as I thought this, I saw the forms of both as I had often pictured them in my mind. I looked at them closely and discovered that they were not realities, but mere shadowy forms in my thoughts, and that any form might be brought up in the same way. What a wonderful world, I exclaimed mentally, where the thought is so intensified as to take visible form. How happy shall I be in such a realm of thought as that.

I listened at the archways for any sound of voice or music, but could hear nothing. Solid substances, I thought, are better media of sound than air. I will use the rocks as media. I rose and placed my left ear to first one rock, and then the other, but could hear nothing.

Then suddenly I was tempted to cross the boundary line. I hesitated and reasoned thus: 'I have died once and if I go back, sooner or later, I must die again. If I stay someone else will do my work, and so the end will be well and as surely accomplished, and shall I die again? I will not, but now that I am so near I will cross the line and stay.' I moved cautiously along the rocks. There was danger of falling over the side of the road, for the pathway around was but narrow. I thought not of the archways, placed my back against the rock and walked sideways.

I reached the exact centre of the rock, which I knew by a carved knob in the rock marking the exact boundary. Here, like Caesar at the Rubicon, I halted and parlayed with conscience. It seems like taking a good deal of responsibility, but I determined to do it, and advanced the left foot across the line. As I did so, a small, densely black cloud appeared in front of me and advanced toward my face. I knew that I was to be stopped. I felt the power to move or think leaving me. My hands fell powerless at my side, my shoulders and head dropped forward, the cloud touched my face, and I knew no more.

Without previous thought and without apparent effort on my part my eyes opened. I looked at my hands, and then at the little white cot upon which I was lying, and realizing that I was in the body, in astonishment and disappointment, I exclaimed: 'What in the world has happened to me? Must I die again?'

I was extremely weak but strong enough to relate the above experience, despite all injunctions to quiet.[18]

Within eight weeks after his 'death', Dr Wiltse made a complete recovery. Every point in his story that could be verified was true.

2. Are the Experiences Real?

Extraordinary as these stories of suspended animation are, they are by no means unusual. Similar stories have been known and collected since ancient times.

In his *Natural History* Pliny says that the ex-consul Aviola came to life on his own funeral pyre, and was roasted alive, because the heat of the flames was already too intense for anyone to be able to rescue him. The same fate befell the ex-praetor Lucius Lamia, but Gaius Aelius Tubero, also an ex-praetor, was said by Messala Rufus and others to have been rescued. Heraclides wrote an essay on a woman restored to life after seven days.

Marcus Varro reports that when he was apportioning lands at Capua as one of the twenty commissioners, a person he saw being carried to his funeral returned home on foot. He says that the same thing happened at Aquino, and that his maternal aunt's husband Corfidus not only came to life at his own funeral, but lived to arrange the funeral of the relative who had originally arranged his.

Agrippa says:

In times of pestilence many that are carried for dead to the graves to be buried revive again. The same also hath often befell women by reason of fits of the mother. And Rabbi Moises, out of the Book of Galen, which Patriarcha translated, makes mention of a man who was suffocated for six days, and did neither eat nor drink, and [whose] arteries became hard. And it is said in that same book, that a certain man, being filled with water, lost the pulse of his whole body, so that the heart was not perceived to move, and he lay like a dead man. It is also said that a man, by reason of a fall from a high place, or great noise, or long staying under the water, may fall into a swoon, which may continue forty-eight hours, and so may lay as if he were dead, his face being very green. And in the same place there is mention made of a man that buried a man, who seemed to be dead, seventy-two hours after his seeming decease, and so killed him because he buried him alive; and there are no given signs whereby it may be known who are alive, although they seem to be dead.

Although it be hard to be believed, we read in some approved historians, that some men have slept for years altogether, and in the time of sleep until they awakened, there was no alteration in them so as to make them seem older. The same doth Pliny testify of a certain boy, whom, he said, being wearied with heat and his journey, slept fifty-seven years in a cave. We read also that Epimenides Gnosius slept fifty-seven years in a cave. Hence the proverb arose, to outsleep Epimenides. M. Damascenus tells us that in his time a certain countryman in Germany, being wearied, slept for the space of a whole autumn and the winter following under a heap of hay, until the summer, when the hay began to be eaten up. Then he was found awakened as a man half dead and out of his wits. Ecclesiastical histories confirm this opinion concerning the seven sleepers, whom they say slept 196 years. There was in Norvegia a cave in a high sea shore, where seven men lay sleeping a long time without corruption. Marcus Damascenus proves it, by many reasons, to be possible and natural, neither doth he think it irrational that some should, without meat and drink, avoiding excitements, and without consuming or corruption, sleep many months. And this may befall a man by reason of some poisonous potion, or sleepy disease, or like such causes, for certain days, months, or years, according to the intention or remission of the power of the medicine, or of the passions of their mind.

If these accounts are true, the dying souls must sometimes, lying hid in their bodies, be oppressed with vehement extasies [sic] and be freed from all bodily action; so that the life, sense, and motion forsake the body, and also that the man is not truly dead, but lies astonied, and [seemingly] dead, as it were, for a certain time. This is the manner by which we understand Magicians and physicians do raise dead men to life.[1]

Eliphas Levi delivers himself of the same opinion. 'Nature', he says, 'accomplishes nothing by sudden jerks, and eternal death is always preceded by a state which partakes somewhat of the nature of lethargy. It is a torpor which a great shock or the magnetism of a powerful will can overcome.' As an example, he mentions the case of the dead man who was resuscitated by being thrown upon the bones of Elisha. 'He explains it by saying that the soul was hovering at that moment near the body', says Madame Blavatsky. 'The burial party, according to tradition, were attacked by robbers, and their fright, communicating itself sympathetically to it, the soul was seized with horror at the idea of its remains being desecrated, and "re-entered violently into its body to raise and save it".' The theologians 'attributed the resuscitation to contact with the bones of Elisha', Levi explains, 'and worship of relics dates logically from this epoch.'[2]

'We may conceive that such kinds of extasies [sic] may continue a long time,' says Agrippa, 'although a man be not truly dead, as it is in door mice and crocodiles and many other serpents, which sleep all winter, and are in such a dead sleep that they can scarce be awakened with fire. I have often seen a door mouse dissected, and continue immovable, as if she were dead, until she was boiled, and when put into boiling water the dissected members did show life.'[3]

If this interpretation is correct, then there is no difference between the experiences of yogis practising suspended animation and those described by men who have 'died' and been resuscitated. This is particularly interesting, because both yogis and the resuscitated 'dead' believe that they have seen extraterrestrial realms of existence.

Sometimes the experiences are vague. Arthur Symons describes just such an experience during surgery in which he felt that he had died. First, there was 'choking and stifling', he says. After that

had passed away, I seemed at first in a state of utter blankness. Then came flashes of intense light, alternating with blackness, and with a keen vision of what was going on in the room around me, but no sensation of touch, I thought that I was near death, when, suddenly, my soul became aware of God, who was manifestly dealing with me, handling me, so to speak, in an intense personal reality. I felt him streaming in *like light upon me* . . . I cannot describe the ecstasy I felt. Then, as I gradually awoke from the influence of the anaesthetics, the old sense of my relation to the world began to return, and the new sense of my relation to God began to fade. I suddenly leaped to my feet 'on the chair where I was sitting, and shrieked out, 'It is too horrible, it is too horrible', meaning that I could not bear this disillusionment. Then I flung myself on the ground and at last awoke covered with blood, calling to the two surgeons (who were frightened) 'Why did you not kill me? Why would you not let me die?'[4]

During the Sicilian War one Gabienus, reputed to be the bravest man in Caesar's navy, was taken prisoner by Sextus Pompeius, who ordered his throat to be cut. The man appeared to be dead, and lay all day on the shore where he had been slain. That evening, he came back to life as it were, and announced to the crowd that he had returned from the *lower world* with a message for Pompey. The gods, he said, had approved Pompey's quarrel with Octavian, and would turn the battle to his favour. He had been sent, he said, to deliver this message, and, upon doing so, died a second time, this time for good. The prophecy was fulfilled, just as he had predicted.[5]

In many cases, the temporarily dead returned with stories which were very elaborate indeed. Such was the case with Er the Pamphylian, whose story Plato tells in the tenth book of his *Republic*. Plutarch tells a similar story about Thespesius, and 'there were endless others', says Vittorio, among whom we might include Cleonimus, Eurinus, Rufus, Hieronymus, Machates, Cleodimus, and Empedotimus. He says that 'the same things were told' about each of these men, and that 'nobody ever doubted that they died, entered a real world of after-life, and then were resurrected'.[6]

The only problem is whether the experiences are real or mere fantasies.

The most common argument offered by those hostile to the notion of an other world is that near death experiences are wish-fulfillment fantasies. The theory is that dying people do not want to die, and rather than face reality, they simply cook up an 'afterlife' for themselves in visionary form. The only problem with this argument is that the wish being fulfilled is not for a life on some *other* plane of existence, but for continued life on this one. A person having a wish-fulfillment fantasy type vision would 'see' himself being saved from death and thereby enabled to continue living in *this* world.

A more interesting argument is that the experiences are induced by the drugs given to dying patients by their physicians. There are several problems with this one, though. In the first place, 'near death experiences' have come down to us from ancient times – from before the drugs in question were first synthesized. Moreover, there is no similarity between the NDE and experiences which are *known* to be drug induced.

We have inherited numerous interesting descriptions of drug

experiences from those who participated in the so-called 'anaesthetic revelation' in the last century. One of these was Xenos Clark, a 'philosopher' who died at Amherst, New York, in the 1880s. He published several books on the use of anaesthetics to produce 'mystical' experiences, and although we may disagree with him on the value of the experiences themselves, there is little doubt that he described them well.

He says that the 'revelation' is

utterly flat, non-emotional . . . It is, as Mr Blood says, 'the one sole and sufficient insight why, or not why but how, the present is pushed on by the past, and sucked forward by the vacuity of the future. Its inevitableness defeats all attempts at stopping or accounting for it. It is all precedence, and presupposition, and questioning is in regard to it forever too late. It is an *initiation of the past*.' The real secret would be the formula by which the 'now' keeps exfoliating out of itself, yet never escapes. What is it, indeed, that keeps existence exfoliating? The formal being of anything, the logical definition of it, is static. For mere logic every question contains its own answer – we simply fill the hole with the dirt we dug out. Why are twice two four? Because, in fact, four is twice two. Thus logic finds in life no propulsion, only a momentum. It goes because it is a-going. But the revelation adds: it goes because it is and was a-going. You walk, as it were, round yourself in the revelation. Ordinary philosophy is like a hound hunting his own trail. The more he hunts, the farther he has to go, and the nose never catches up with his heels, because it is forever ahead of them. So the present is already a foregone conclusion, and I am ever too late to understand it. But at the moment of recovery from anesthesis [sic], just then, *before starting on life*, I catch, so to speak, a glimpse of my heels, a glimpse of the eternal process just in the act of starting. The truth is that we travel on a journey that was accomplished before we set out; and the real end of philosophy is accomplished, not when we arrive at, but when we remain in, our destination (being already there), which may occur vicariously in this life when we cease our intellectual questioning. That is why there is a smile upon the face of the revelation, as we view it. It tells us that we are forever half a second too late – that's all. "You could kiss your own lips and have all the fun to yourself", it says, if you only knew the trick. It would be perfectly easy if they would just manage to stay there till you got round to them. Why don't you manage it somehow?[7]

It is obvious that this is far from the near death experience, or any of the experiences related by astral projectors or suspended animators. James, who tells this story, has another story which is worth quoting, and which comes from an Englishwoman, 'gifted', as James says, but obviously on a different intellectual plane from Mr Clark.

Unlike Clark and his friends, this woman was not an experimenter with the anaesthetic revelation. Her experience just came to her during surgery, in a transient moment between sleep and waking.

My last dream immediately preceded my real coming to. It only lasted a few seconds, and was most vivid and real to me, though it may not be clear in words.

A great Being or Power was travelling through the sky. His foot was on a kind of lightning as a wheel is upon a railway. It was his pathway. The lightning was made entirely of the spirits of innumerable people close to one another, and I was one of them. He moved in a straight line, and each part of the streak or flash came into its short conscious existence only that he might travel. I seemed to be directly under the foot of God, and I thought that he was grinding his own life up out of my pain. Then I saw that what he had been trying with all his might to do was to *change his course*, to *bend* the line of lightning to which he was tied, in the direction in which he wanted to go. I felt my flexibility and helplessness, and knew that he would succeed. He bended me, turning his corner by means of my hurt, hurting me more than I had ever been hurt in my life, and at the acutest moment of this, as he passed, I *saw*. I understood for a moment things that I have now forgotten, things that no one could remember while retaining sanity. The angle was an obtuse angle, and I remember thinking as I woke that had he made it a right or acute angle, I should have 'seen' still more, and should probably have died.[8]

Anyone who has ever suffered from high fever will recognize this instantly as an excellent description of delirium – the psychic product of an overheated brain. Once again, however, there is no resemblance to any kind of astral projection experience, and certainly not to the NDE.

For dreams of a different sort we can turn to De Quincey in his *Confessions of an English Opium-Eater*. Having taken massive overdoses of laudanum for several years, he says

I seemed every night to descend, not metaphorically, but literally to descend into chasms and sunless abysses, depths below depths, from which it seemed hopeless that I could ever reascend. Nor did I, by waking, feel that I *had* reascended. For indeed the state of gloom which attended these gorgeous spectacles, amounting at last to utter darkness, as of some suicidal despondency, cannot be approached by words.

Afterwards came

dreams of lakes and silvery expanses of water . . . . The waters gradually changed their character – from translucent lakes, shining like mirrors, they became seas and oceans. And now came a tremendous change, which, unfolding itself slowly like a scroll, through many months, promised an abiding torment . . . . Upon the rocking waters of the ocean the human face began to reveal itself. The sea appeared paved with innumerable faces, upturned to the heavens. Faces imploring, wrathful, despairing. Faces that surged upwards by thousands, by myriads, by generations . . . . My mind tossed, as it seemed, upon the billowy ocean, and weltered upon the weltering waves.[9]

Other dreams concerned visions of ages past, of balls in the time of Charles I, of crocodiles and Egyptian temples. *Hashish*, it is said, whisks its users away to the closest thing to paradise that can be experienced on earth, and the Old Man of the Mountain used it to make fanatics of his young Muslim warriors. But like the delirious experience described above, and the anaesthetic revelation, none of these dreams bears any resemblance to either astral projection or to the NDE. That said, let us look at the astral projection experience and see what it tells us.

From the mystical point of view, nothing is 'real' except 'Reality' itself. This world we live in is mere illusion, or *Maya*, a phantasmagoria of shifting images which have no real existence outside the dreams of the cosmic consciousness. The same thing is true of the superphysical realms, according to this philosophy.

To the man in the street, though – and I include myself in this category – the world is real enough, and the definition of the word 'real' must somehow use the world as a basis. Therefore, when we ask whether or not the astral plane is real, we mean 'real' in the sense that the world is real. It does not matter whether or not *anything* is real mystically if we use this yardstick.

Now philosophers will say that the world is real because we experience it, and in that sense anything else that we may experience, including dreams and hallucinations, is also real. That forces us to refine our problem somewhat, and define *two* types of reality – social and non-social. A dream is real to you since you experience it, but it is not real to anyone else. Hence, it is a non-social reality. It belongs only to a single owner, whereas a speeding automobile, which will become rapidly real to anyone who stands in its way, is a social reality. The problem, then, is to determine whether astral projection experiences are realities in the social, and not the mystical, sense, and that simplifies everything.

The psychic research term for 'real' is 'veridical', which means 'truth-telling', and there are two accepted criteria for determining whether a projection experience is 'veridical' or not. The projector must make his presence felt by some naïve observer at a distant place, or else he must return from his trip with some knowledge that he could not have acquired except by psychic means. Either of these conditions is considered sufficient to establish veridicality. If neither condition is met, the experience is a fantasy.

Augustine mentions a man who 'declared that in his own house at night, before he slept, he saw a certain philosopher, whom he knew very well, come and explain to him some things in the Platonic philosophy which he had previously declined to explain when asked. And when he asked this philosopher why he did in his house what he refused to do at home, he said, "I did not do it, but I *dreamed* I had done it." 'And thus,' says the saint, 'what the one saw when sleeping was shown to the other when awake by a phantasmal image.' He says that 'these things have not come to us from persons we might deem worthy of credit, but from informants we could not suppose to be deceiving us.'[10] There is hardly any question that he is right, because there are numerous other stories of the same type.

One of the most amazing appears in Jung-Stilling's *Pneumatology*.

In the neighbourhood of Philadelphia there dwelt a solitary man in a lonely house. He was very benevolent, but extremely retired and reserved, and strange things were related of him, amongst which were his being able to tell a person things that were unknown to everyone else. Now it happened, that the captain of a vessel belonging to Philadelphia was about to sail to Asia and Europe. He promised his wife that he would return again in a certain time, and also that he would write to her frequently. She waited long, but no letters arrived. The time appointed passed over, but her beloved husband did not return. She was now deeply distressed, and knew not where to go for counsel or consolation. At length, a friend advised her to go to the pious solitary, and tell him her griefs. The woman followed his advice, and went to him. After she told him all her troubles, he desired her to wait awhile there, until he returned and brought her an answer. She sat down to wait, and the man, opening a door, went into his closet. But the woman, thinking he stayed a long time, rose up, went to the window of the door, lifted up the little curtain, and looking in, saw him lying on the couch or sofa like a corpse. She then immediately went back to her place. At length he came and told her that her husband was in London, in a coffee-house which he named, and that he would return very soon. He then told her the reason why he had been unable to write. The woman went home pretty much at ease.

What the solitary told her was minutely fulfilled. Her husband returned, and the reasons of his delay and his not writing were just the same as the man had stated. The woman was now curious to know what would be the result if she visited the friendly solitary in company with her husband. The visit was arranged, but when the captain saw the man he was struck with amazement. He afterwards told his wife that he had seen this very man the very day the woman had been with him in a coffee-house in London, that he had told him that his wife was much distressed about him, that he had then stated the reason why his return was delayed, and of his not writing, and that he would shortly come back, on which he lost sight of the man among the company.[11]

In his *German Pietists of Provincial Pennsylvania*, Julius Sachse identifies the 'pious solitary' as Conrad Matthai, a member of the Pennsylvania Rosicrucian colony.[12] He would therefore have had some training in this sort of thing, which explains why he could do it at will. In any event, it is clear that both of the two conditions for veridicality are met here. Matthai brought back information he could not have obtained, except psychically, and he made his presence felt in the most emphatic manner. We may not understand how it works, but that astral travel is possible seems to be beyond doubt – at least in this world. As we shall soon see, it is also possible in the next.

3. Swedenborg

Emmanuel Swedenborg was undoubtedly the most extraordinary psychic in history, and he is of particular interest to us here, because not only did he peer into the farthest regions of the astral plane, and not only did he furnish evidence that astral plane experiences are real, but he left us some of the most complete descriptions of what he saw there.

Even though he lived in Sweden, he seems to have adopted London as a second home of sorts, and it was in 1745 while he was in that city that his career as a seer began.

> I was one day dining very late at my hotel in London, and I ate with great appetite, when at the end of my repast I perceived a sort of fog which obstructed my view, and the floor was covered with hideous reptiles. They disappeared, the darkness was dispersed, and I plainly saw, in the midst of a bright light, a man sitting in the corner of my room, who said in a terrible voice, *Do not eat so much*. At these words my sight was bedimmed, but I regained it little by little, and then found that I was alone.

The following night, he saw the man again, and was told – or *thought* he was told – that the 'man' was really God. Somehow I doubt that, but the experience had an extraordinary psychic effect on him nonetheless. He says that 'this very night the eyes of my *interior* were opened and enabled me to see into Heaven, into the World of Spirits, into Hell, in which places I found many of my acquaintances, some who had been long since dead, others only a short time.'[1] Those visions were to continue until his death in 1772.

Now visions of 'hideous reptiles' are typical of *delirium tremens*, and Barruel, who relates this story, says that 'this vision would appear more worthy of a man to whom one might say in a less terrible voice, "Do not *drink* so much.'' [2] We could leave it at that were it not for the fact that Swedenborg seems subsequently to have demonstrated real clairvoyance.

Myers, the famous British psychic researcher, has observed that Swedenborg's testimony concerning the so-called spirit-world 'is in substantial accord with what has been given through the most trustworthy sensitives since Swedenborg's time.' [3] One could, of course, assume that Swedenborg *influenced* these later sensitives, just as one could explain similarities between Swedenborg's testimony and that of earlier travellers by saying that they influenced him. But we now know that he is corroborated by *The Tibetan Book of the Dead* in numerous important respects. And surely his fame could not have spread to such a remote and primitive country. According to ancient principle, when two or more witnesses agree that they saw such and such a thing at such and such a place, and it is established that they could not have colluded in preparing their story, their veracity is proved. But where the astral plane is concerned, we need more, and with Swedenborg we seem to get it.

The first incident we shall consider was reported by Immanuel Kant in a letter to Charlotte von Knobloch dated 10 August 1763. The German text of the letter is appended to several editions of Kant's *Dreams of a Spirit-Seer*, which was written several years later, and probably caused the philosopher considerable embarrassment since he wished publicly to avoid being tarnished with the tar-brush of the occult. I give the story in Kant's own words.

> The following occurrence appears to me to have above all the greatest proof and really confounds every recognizable doubt or excuse. It was in the year 1756, toward the end of September on a Saturday at 4 o'clock in the afternoon, when Herr von Swedenborg arrived at Gothenburg from England. Herr William Castel invited him to his house together with a party of fifteen other persons. That evening at six o'clock Her von Swedenborg left and came back to the gathering room looking pale and disturbed. He said that just then a dangerous fire was burning in Stockholm at the Suedermalm (Gothenburg is more than fifty miles from Stockholm) and that it was spreading rapidly. He was restless and went out frequently. He said that the house of one of his friends, whom he named, was already in ashes, and that his own house was in danger. At eight o'clock, after he had been out again, he said joyfully. ''Thank God, the fire is extinguished the third door from my house!'' – This news brought the entire city, and especially his own party, to a great commotion,

and someone told the governor the news that same evening. Sunday morning Swedenborg was summoned repeatedly by the governor, who questioned him about the incident. Swedenborg described the fire precisely, how it began, how it ended, and how long it burned. The same day, the news spread throughout the entire city, where it caused greater consternation because of the governor's interest, and because many feared for their friends or goods. On Monday evening a messenger came to Gothenburg, who was despatched during the fire by the Kaufmannstadt in Stockholm. The letters he brought described the fire exactly like [Swedenborg's] story. On Tuesday Morning a royal courier came to the governor with an account of the fire, the loss, and the damage to housing that it had caused, not in the least differing from the narrative that Swedenborg had given at the time it happened. Moreover the fire had indeed been extinguished at 8 o'clock.

What can anyone bring forward against the creditworthiness of this story? The friend who wrote this to me sought out everything, not only in Stockholm, but about two months ago in Gothenburg, where he knew some of the prominent families well, and where he could get complete information, since most of the eyewitnesses are still alive there, 1756 being such a short time ago.[4]

Another such story is given by Jung-Stilling, an early German psychic researcher.

In 1762, on the very day when the Emperor Peter III of Russia died, Swedenborg was present with me at a party in Amsterdam. In the middle of a conversation, his physiognomy became changed, and it was evident that his soul was no longer present in him, and that something was taking place within him. As soon as he recovered he was asked what had happened. At first he would not speak, but after being repeatedly urged, he said, 'Now, at this very hour, the Emperor Peter has died in prison,' explaining the nature of his death. 'Gentlemen, will you please make a note of this day, in order that you may compare it with the announcement of his death which will appear in the newspapers. The papers soon after announced the death of the Emperor which had taken place on the very same day.[5]

Both of these stories indicate plainly that Swedenborg had a genuine, albeit spontaneous, ability to do astral projection. He even describes the experience in his books, and in language that no eighteenth-century gentleman could have used without firsthand knowledge of the subject. He says that he would be 'brought to a certain state' which he describes as 'intermediate between sleep and wakefulness.' 'A person in this state,' he says, 'cannot know but that he is quite awake,' since 'all the senses are as much awake as in the completest state of bodily vigilance, the sight as well as the hearing, and, what is remarkable, the touch, which is then more exquisite than it can ever be in bodily wakefulness . . . and [yet] almost nothing of the body then intervenes.'[6]

Sometimes he says the 'state' came to him while 'walking through the streets of a city and through the country.' He would be 'in conversation with spirits', as he thought, and 'in a vision, seeing groves, rivers, palaces, houses, men, and many other objects.' After several hours like this, 'suddenly I was in bodily vision,' as distinguished from psychic vision, 'and observed that I was in a different place.'[7]

Now all of this serves to establish that Swedenborg could project on this plane, but that does not really interest us here. What *does* interest us is whether he could project into *other* planes of existence, or, for that matter, whether there *are* any other planes of existence into which he could have projected. Swedenborg maintains that he could, he did, and there are, and, based on other stories, it would seem that he was right.

The most famous of these is, of course, the story of the 'Queen's letter'. Queen Lovisa Ulrika of Sweden had become interested in Swedenborg's unusual gifts, which were apparently the subject of much conversation in those days, and, like Herod with Christ, invited him to appear at her court and perhaps perform some wonder. The royal summons was delivered to the seer in the fall of 1761 by Count Ulric Scheffer, who accompanied him to the royal presence. According to Barruel, the Queen asked Swedenborg to find out why her brother Augustus William, the Prince of Prussia, had died without answering a certain letter which she had written to him. Swedenborg promised to consult the deceased. The following day he returned and addressed himself as follows to the Queen, 'Your brother appeared to me last night, and ordered me to inform you, that he has not answered your letter because he disapproved of your conduct, because your imprudent politics and your ambition were the cause of the effusion of blood. I command you, therefore, in his name to meddle no more in state affairs, and particularly not any more to excite troubles to which you would, sooner or later, fall the victim.' The Queen was astonished, as she well might have been. Not only did lesser mortals not go around 'commanding' queens to do anything, but Barruel says that 'Swedenborg told her things that she alone and the deceased could know, and the reputation of the prophet was much increased.'[8]

Now it must be said that Swedenborg's detractors were not silent on this question, and in the January 1788 edition of the *Berliner Monatschrifft* a prominent German anti-mystic named Rollig offered a theory about what *could* have happened. He suggested that the Queen's letter 'had been intercepted by two Senators', who disclosed its contents to the seer, and 'who profited of this occasion to give her the above lesson through the medium of Swedenborg.'[9] According to Barruel, who relates this story, 'when the disciples of Swedenborg saw this letter appear, they gave a new turn to the story. It was no longer the Queen questioning Swedenborg about the letter. She simply asked *whether he had seen her brother?* Swedenborg is said at the end of a week to return to the Queen, and tell her things that she believed herself alone conversant with, after the decease of the prince. This contrivance gives a whole week to prepare the trick.'[10]

Of course this is mere speculation, and assumes that Swedenborg was capable, not only of fraud, but of fraud directed against his sovereign, for whom he had great respect. Moreover, the theory only seems to have been credited by Rollig, who was an anti-mystic, and Barruel, who was a priest promoting a rival church. Immanuel Kant, who investigated this question rather thoroughly, makes it clear that everyone else, particularly in Sweden, believed the miracle was genuine.

Kant heard this story 'through a Danish officer, who was my friend and a former student.' The officer was at dinner with Dietrichstein, the Austrian Ambassador to Copenhagen, and several other guests, when he was invited to read a letter which the Ambassador had recently received from the Baron de Lutzow, the Mecklenburg Ambassador to Stockholm. In it the Baron asserts that he was personally at the court of the Queen in company with the Dutch Ambassador when Swedenborg made his appearance, and that he was therefore an eyewitness to this extraordinary incident. Kant wrote:

The credibility of such an account surprises me. One can hardly assume that an Ambassador should write a story to another Ambassador, *for open use*, which has to do with the Queen of the Court where he finds himself, which involves matters which took place while he was present with a distinguished company, and which is untrue. In order not to blindly discard a prejudice against

apparitions and visions in favour of a new prejudice, I found it logical
to inquire into this history more closely. I wrote to the aforementioned
officer at Copenhagen and asked him several questions. He answered
that he had again spoke to the Grafen von Dietrichstein concerning
this matter, that the matter really stood as related, and that Professor
Schlegel had told him that it was thereby in no manner to be doubted.
He advised me, since he was about to go to the army under General St
Germain, to write to Swedenborg myself, and learn more of the
particulars that way. I wrote to Swedenborg, and the letter was
handed him by an English merchant in Stockholm. I learned that
Herr von Swedenborg received the letter politely and said that he
would reply. This was the only answer I never [sic] received. Mean-
while I made the acquaintance of a cultivated man, an Englishman who
spent last summer here, and, on the strength of the friendship which
brought us together, commissioned him to learn something of Herr
von Swedenborg's miracles when he went to Stockholm. His first
letter confirms the story as reported, and on the authority of the most
respectable people in Stockholm. He had not yet spoken with Herr
von Swedenborg himself, but hoped to do so, yet was unable to
believe that all of this about his secret communications with the
invisible spirit-world, which was told by the most reasonable persons
of the city, was true. His following letters were altogether different.
He has not only spoken to Herr von Swedenborg, but visited at his
house, and is in the greatest amazement concerning the entire
aforementioned matter. Swedenborg is a reasonable, polite, and
open-hearted man. He is learned, and my friend has promised to send
me some of his writings shortly. [Swedenborg] said this without
reservation, that God had given him this peculiar gift of communicating
with departed souls when he wished. He supported this with all the
notorious facts. Reminded of my letter, he answered that he had
certainly received it, and would have already answered it, were it not
that he intended to open this whole singular matter to the eyes of the
world. He would go to London in May of this year, where he would
publish a book in which a reply to my letter on every article would be
given.

Kant also tells one other tale of Swedenborg's ability to speak with
the dead, which, unlike the story about the Queen's letter, does not lend
itself to *any* fraudulent explanation at all. He says that 'the whole living
public is witness' to this event, and that 'the man who reported it to me

investigated it at the place where it happened.'

Madame Harteville, the widow of the Dutch Envoy to Stockholm, was asked by the goldsmith Croon, some time after her husband's death, to pay for a silver service he had ordered. The widow was convinced that her late husband had been too neat and orderly not to have paid the debt, but she could not find the receipt. In this distress, and because the sum was considerable, she summoned Her von Swedenborg. After an apology for his inconvenience, she asked him, if, as everyone said, he had the extraordinary gift of speaking with departed souls, to have the kindness to inquire of her husband how it was with the silver service. Swedenborg was not at all reluctant to grant her request. Three days later the aforementioned lady had company at her house for coffee. Her von Swedenborg came in and told her, in his cold-blooded manner, that he had spoken with her husband. The debt had been paid seven months before his death, and the receipt was in a cupboard to be found in an upper room of the house. The lady averred that the cupboard had been completely emptied, and that the receipt had not been found among the papers. Swedenborg said that her husband had described to him how when a drawer on the left side is pulled out, a plank would appear, which must be pulled out, whereupon a secret compartment would be disclosed, containing his secret bound Dutch correspondence, and the receipt as well. On hearing this the lady proceeded, accompanied by all her guests, to the upper room. The drawer was opened and, proceeding exactly as described, the plank was found, which no one knew of before, and the aforementioned papers therein, to the greatest astonishment of everyone present.

Now Swedenborg himself did not consider his psychic experiences very important, and he did not place much emphasis on his descriptions of the astral plane. What *he* thought was important was a new system of theology he was trying to promote, and which he claimed was validated by his visionary experiences. Modern critics tend to feel just the opposite.

Myers says of Swedenborg's 'dogmatic' writings that they 'have appeared more and more to be mere fantasies, mere projections and repercussions of his own preconceived ideas.'[11] It was moreover these 'dogmatic' writings, which consisted of private interpretations of the Bible, and not his psychic experiences, which motivated most of his rivals in the religious marketplace to try to cast doubt on his integrity. Hence, when Swedenborg was dying in London, about the Christmas of 1771, he was visited by a minister of the Lutheran Church in London, one M. Ferelius. Ferelius recalled later,

> I asked him if he thought he was going to die and he answered in the affirmative, upon which I requested him, since many believed that he had invented his new system merely to acquire a great name (which he had certainly obtained), to take this opportunity of proclaiming the whole truth to the world, and to recant either wholly or in part what he had advanced, especially as his pretensions could now be of no further use to him. Upon this Swedenborg raised himself up in bed, and placing his hand upon his breast, said with earnestness, 'Everything that I have written is as true as you now behold me. I might have said much more had it been permitted to me. After death you will see all, and then we shall have much to say to each other on this subject.' [12]

He never doubted that his ability to project onto the astral plane was genuine. Shortly afterwards he joined the spirits with whom he had spent his life, and was buried in a Swedish church at Ratclif highway.

4. Astral Sex

Once upon a time, in the district of Gareotha, some fourteen miles from Aberdeen in Scotland, a young man was haunted by the ghost of a woman, 'more beautiful than any woman that he had ever seen.' She came to his rooms by night, passing through locked doors and shuttered windows, and 'coaxed and forced him', as Guazzo says, to have sexual intercourse with her. All night long she would use the young man to satisfy her passion, then depart at the break of dawn, 'with scarcely any sound', only to return the following night.[1]

In the city of Bonn, in Germany, lived a Catholic priest named Arnold, who had a daughter of exceptional beauty. He was exceedingly jealous of the girl's virginity, and preserved her by locking her in an upstairs room whenever he left his house. One evening he returned from service to his parishioners to find the girl in tears. When asked what was the matter, she told him that a spirit had attended her, foiling both bars and locks, and that he had made love to her, despite all her efforts at resistance.[2]

Still another story concerns a girl of noble lineage who lived in the vicinity of Moray Firth in Scotland. She refused several noblemen who asked to marry her, and, upon being asked why by her parents, said that she had 'a marvellously beautiful youth' who 'had frequent intercourse with her by night, and sometimes by day.' She said that 'she did not know whence he came or whither he went', but he had, as Guazzo put it, 'stormed the fortress of [her] virginity' successfully. Three days after this remarkable revelation, one of the maids heard the pair making love and informed her parents that the youth, *whoever* he was, was with her. They locked and bolted the house so that he could not escape, threw open the door to the girl's room, and found her with a Being of unearthly appearance.[3]

Sprenger says that in his time women were sometimes surprised in the fields and woods, lying on the ground, naked from the waist down, moaning and writhing as if having sexual intercourse, yet without any visible lover being present. After a time, 'a black vapour of the size of a man' would be seen to depart from the girl 'and to ascend from that place'.[4]

These stories are typical of what one might call erotic hauntings. They are ghost stories, but they differ from other ghost stories in that the ghost seems to want more than just to hang about uninvited. In Japan these ghosts are known as 'Yoku-shiki-gaki', or 'spirits of lewdness'. *Gaki* is the Japanese equivalent of the Indian word *Preta*, the earthbound spirit of a mortal who did not, for some reason, ascend to the World of Boundless Light, and who, while awaiting reincarnation, not only clings to the earth-sphere, but seeks out erotic encounters. Says Lafcadio Hearn:

> They can change their sex at will and can make their bodies as large or small as they please. It is impossible to exclude them from any dwelling, except by the use of holy charms or spells, since they are able to pass through an orifice even smaller than the eye of a needle. To seduce young men, they assume beautiful feminine shapes – often appearing at wine-parties as waitresses or dancing girls. To seduce women they take the form of handsome lads. This state of Yoku-shiki-gaki is a consequence of lust in some previous human existence, but the supernatural powers belonging to their condition are results of meritorious Karma which the evil Karma could not wholly counterbalance.[5]

In ancient times it was believed that these erotic ghosts were capable, not only of making love, but of siring children.

Geoffrey of Monmouth tells just such a story about Merlin, which has been repeated by all the chroniclers since. Merlin's mother was the daughter of King Demetius, and a nun – thus a royal virgin. When King Vortigern asked her the name of her son's father, she said 'that she had never enjoyed the society of any mortal or human, but only spirit, assuming the shape of a beautiful young man. The spirit 'had many times appeared unto her, seeking to court her with no common affection, but when any of her fellow-virgins came in, he would suddenly disappear and vanish. [After] many and urgent importunities, I yielded, saith she, to his pleasure – and I was delivered of this son (now in your presence) whom I caused to be called Merlin.'[6]

Christopher Heywood, who is one of Merlin's biographers, admits that 'this may be easily believed to be a mere fiction . . . to conceal the person of her sweetheart . . . And yet,' he says, 'we read that the other fantastical congression is not impossible.'

'For Speusippus, the son of Plato's sister, and Elearchus the Sophist, and Amaxilides, in the second book of his philosophy, affirm in the honour of Plato, that his mother, Perictione, having congression with the imaginary shadow of Apollo, conceived and brought into the world him who proved to be the prince of philosophers.'[7]

Apollo was imagined by the ancients to be a real womanizer. In his *Life of Alexander*, Plutarch says that before Alexander was born, Philip of Macedon peeked at his mother Olympias through a chink in the door to her bedroom and saw her lying with a serpent. He sent Chaeron of Megalopolis to the Oracle of Delphi to learn the significance of the vision, and was told that the serpent was the god Apollo, and that the god had been having sexual intercourse with Olympias at the moment when Philip caught them. The oracle said that Philip was doomed to lose the eye with which he committed that impiety, and that Olympias would give birth to a son who would be only half mortal.[3]

Apollo was positively chaste in comparison to Zeus who the ancients thought was out to ravish every girl in sight, whether goddess or mortal. Bacchus was the son of Zeus and a mortal woman named Semele, the princess of Thebes. Perseus was the son of Zeus and the virgin Danae, princess of Argos. Amphion was the son of Zeus and Antiope, princess of Boeotia. Mercury was the son of Zeus and Maia, the daughter of Atlas, and a similar origin was claimed for Aeolus, Arcas, Aroclus, and even Apollo himself.[9]

In her *Esoteric Philosophy of Love and Marriage*, published by the Aquarian Press, Dion Fortune offers an interesting theory which *could* explain how such legends got started.

She says that according to 'esoteric philosophy' man has seven 'bodies', and not just one, and that 'sex, or polarity', exists on 'each of the seven planes according to their several conditions.' All seven of these 'bodies' are sexual, then, and not just the physical body, and 'unless a man mates each of his bodies which has arrived at a functional state, his state of union will be incomplete, and he will still be in a state of sex-hunger, seeking his mate.'[10]

During the act of mating, she says, 'the subtle forces of the two natures rush together, and, as in the case of two currents of water in collision, a whirlpool or vortex is set up.'[11] In *Psychic Self Defence* she describes this 'psychic vortex' as 'resembling a waterspout, a funnel-shaped swirling that towers up into other dimensions'.

> As body after body engages, the vortex goes up the plane . . . . A soul upon the astral plane may be drawn into the vortex if it is ripe for incarnation, and thus enter the sphere of its parents. If the vortex extends higher than the astral plane, souls of a different type may enter this sphere, but such extension is rare, and therefore it is said that man is born of desire, for few are born of anything else.[12]

If this theory is correct, then the mere fact that someone sheds his physical body at death or during astral projection does not, *ipso facto*, make him a non-sexual being, which is the only objection one could raise to stories of erotic hauntings. That doesn't mean that stories of virgin birth should be accepted as historical fact, but it does suggest that sex continues, not only into old age, but beyond the grave. And it suggests some interesting possibilities for the traveller on the astral plane.

In his *Adventures of a Modern Occultist*, British spiritualist Oliver Bland related several stories of sex in the other world, based on the testimony of 'spirits', breathed a deep late-Victorian sigh, and gave his readers some bad news. He had reached the 'inevitable conclusion', he said, that 'however much we may desire to get rid of it, sex is as troublesome in the next world as in this.'[13]

He says that a great deal of material tended to 'come through' during seances that supported this conclusion, but that it was kept from the public, since Spiritualistic writers wished to portray the spirit-world as a place where sex did not exist. Even Bland felt that 'the accounts could not be published for general or even private reading' but he says frankly that they 'show what may be called a peculiarly active sex-life in the after-world.'[14]

As an example, here are a few words from a Muslim 'spirit' who called himself Sidi Aissa Ben S'dub, and who was evoked by French experimenters in Algiers. Bland describes it as a 'cryptic statement' with which the spirit 'prefaces his words': 'Know, then, O mortals, that here are neither camels nor horses – nor virtuous women – for us, virtue, as ye know it, exists not. And, as I have related, there being neither camels nor horses nor virtuous women, what think ye then occupies the time of us who were strong men?'[15]

Swedenborg is more explicit. He says that 'we are not to infer that celestial couples are unacquainted with voluptuousness,' because 'the propensity to unite exists in the *spiritual* bodies as it does in the material bodies. The angels of both sexes are always in the most perfect state of beauty, youth, and vigour. They enjoy therefore the utmost voluptuousness of conjugal love, and that to a much greater degree than is possible for mortals.'[16]

In *A Magician Among the Spirits*, Houdini tells of a man who lost his wife and became a spiritualist so that he could embrace and fondle her fully materialized form during seances. The presence of other sitters prevented the pair from going any further than just that, but the mediums who invoke such spirits have been known to call them up in private for more intimate encounters.

'If there are "Spirits" capable of drinking tea and wine, of eating apples and cakes, of kissing and touching the visitors of seance rooms, all of which facts have been proven, *why should not those same spirits perform matrimonial duties as well?*', asks Madame Blavatsky.[17] She certainly knew enough examples from her own experience. One was 'an idiotic, old, and slovenly Canadian medium' who believed he had a spirit wife – in life a famous novelist – and that they had bred a 'herd' of spiritual children.[18] Another was 'a well-known New York lady medium' who believed that she had an astral husband – a 'nightly consort', as she put it – and she mentions still others in France.[19]

It was her belief that 'holy spirits will not visit promiscuous seance rooms, nor will they intermarry with living men and women.'[20] The spirits that were doing all this carousing were therefore spirits of a different – unholy – kind, although let it be said that Madame Blavatsky was not a Christian and would have had nothing to do with theological notions of 'devils'. Nonetheless, she believed that these mediums were in danger of 'death and madness' and that several of them 'escaped . . . only by becoming Theosophists. It is only by following our advice that they got finally rid of their spiritual consorts of both sexes.'[21]

Just how to do this, she doesn't say, but Jules Bois does. According to 'a theologian of great erudition' that he consulted, one must 'fumigate the haunted chamber with a melange of pepper, birthwort roots, *cardamoine*, ginger, caryophyllaceous herbs, cinnamon, nutmeg, calamite resin, benzoin, a forest of aloes, and trisanthe.' This is supposed to work against 'aquatic demons'. For others, we are counselled to use water-lily, liverwort, cypress, mandrake, and henbane.[22] In his *Discoverie of Witchcraft*, Reginald Scot says that a common 'cure' for an erotic haunting was to take a stone 'which hath naturally a hole in it', pass a string through the stone, and hang it over the afflicted person's bed.[23]

A more ingenious method was adopted by self-sacrificing Saint Christine. Whenever some lady of her acquaintance was afflicted with an erotic ghost, she would simply sleep in the unfortunate woman's bed, and suffer through the experiences herself.[24]

Daniel Defoe mentions a man who was

> so haunted with naked ladies, fine beautiful ladies in bed with him, and ladies of his acquaintance, too, offering their favours to him, and all in his sleep, that he seldom slept without some such entertainment. The particulars are too gross for my story, but he gave me several long accounts of his night's amours, and being a man of virtuous life and good morals, it was the greatest surprise to him imaginable. He owned with grief to me, that the very first attack was with a very beautiful lady of his acquaintance, who he had been really something freer than ordinary with in their common conversation. This lady [came] to him in a posture for wickedness, and wrought up his inclination so high in his sleep, that he, as he thought, went about actually to debauch her, she not at all resisting, but that he waked at the very moment, to his particular satisfaction.
>
> He was greatly concerned at this part, namely, that he really gave the consent of his will to the fact, and wanted to know if he was guilty of adultery, as if he *had* lain with her. Indeed, he decided the question against himself so forcibly that I, who was of the same opinion, had nothing to say against it.
>
> Nor could all my divinity or his own keep the [succubi] from attacking him again. On the other hand, as I have said, he worried to the degree, that he injured his health, naked women [coming] to him, sometimes one, sometimes another, sometimes in one posture of lewdness, sometimes in another, sometimes into his very arms, sometimes with such additions as I am not merry enough to put into your heads. The man, indeed, could not help it. But as I hinted to him, he might bring his mind to such stated habit of virtue, as to prevent its assenting to any wicked motion, even in sleep, and that would be the way to put an end to the attempt. And this advice he relished very much, and practiced, I believe, with success.[25]

Numerous writers mention this phenomenon of a succuba impersonating some living woman in order to get her way. Brignoli has such a case in his *Alexicacon*.

The incident took place at Bergamo in the year 1650, and the victim – if we can call him that – was a young man, twenty-two years old. He was in bed one night, when the chamber door opened, and a girl named Teresa 'stealthily entered'. She explained that she had been driven from her home, and had come to him for refuge. He was in love with this girl, and when she suggested that they *make* love, he readily assented. Summers says that he 'passed a night of unbounded indulgence in her arms', but that before morning, she revealed her true identity. She was, of course, a succuba. Nonetheless, 'the same debauchery was repeated night after night, until struck with terror and remorse, he sought the priest to confess and be delivered from this abomination.'[26] In the year 1337 a woman named Joan, who lived at Kingsley in the diocese of Winchester, is said to have had a lover, named William. She met him in the forest of Wolmer for romantic purposes, but on seeing him later at a different place, he denied that he had ever been there. She realized that she had made love to an incubus, who had assumed William's form for the purpose, and died soon afterward, or so says the monkish chronicler.[27] In a more amusing case which was left to us by Reginald Scot, an incubus 'came to a lady's bedside and made hot love to her'. She seems to have consented at first, but after he was through, suddenly she took offence, and 'cried out so loud that a company came' and found the ghost hiding under her bed. It looked exactly like Silvanus, the local bishop! Just why a ghost would hide, rather than melt into thin air, as ghosts are wont to do, we cannot imagine, but the incident provoked sniggers all round, and did considerable harm to the bishop's reputation.

Sometimes there is clear evidence of mental pathology in these stories. In his *Autobiographies*, Yeats wrote of his *guru*, MacGregor Mathers, that he 'is much troubled by ladies who seek spiritual advice. One had called to ask his help against phantoms who have the appearance of decayed corpses, and try to get into bed with her at night. He has driven her away with one furious sentence, "Very bad taste on both sides".'[28] If his story is true, though, Mathers must have been in a bad mood when the woman called, because he claimed to know something about this phenomenon and dispensed information on the subject to his Golden Dawn members.

When Dion Fortune published her *Esoteric Philosophy of Love and Marriage*, Mathers' wife Moina almost expelled her from the organization on the grounds that occult sexual information was part of the GD's secret teaching, which she was sworn not to disclose. 'It was pointed out to her that I had not then got the grade in which that teaching was given,' she later wrote, 'and I was pardoned.'[29] However, it is obvious that she must have received this teaching in an irregular manner from some fellow initiate, and thereon hangs a tale.

In *My Rosicrucian Adventure*, Israel Regardie flatly denies that any sexual teaching whatever was given out by the Golden Dawn. 'I have seen most of the important documents issued to the Zelator Adeptus Minor, including a few of those used by the Theoricus Adeptus Minor,' he says, 'and there is nothing in them which could even remotely be interpreted as sex-magic.'[30] But *most* of the important documents is not *all* of the important documents. Mr Regardie is contradicted in this not only by Dion Fortune, but by two other witnesses as well – Catherine Mary Stoddart, and Ithell Colquhoun – and it is probably more than coincidence that all three of these are girls.

Now it must be emphasized here that none of these ladies ever suggested that the GD's sexual theories were ever taught at a *practical*, as opposed to a merely theoretical, level. But it is impossible to believe that such teaching did not exist with all the testimony to the contrary, and one suspects that only women were initiated into it. Ithell Colquhoun says that Westcott and Mathers 'recommended an Elemental marriage' to a Mrs Carden, 'despite the fact that she was married already in a less rarefied fashion to A. J. Carden and had produced a daughter.'[31] And Miss Stoddart says that an initiate known as 'E.O.L.' brought certain breathing exercises to England from lodges in Germany which were supposed to 'arouse and raise the unused sex-forces' for occult purposes.[32] The Germans were quite interested in this problem of how to 'arouse and raise' the 'unused sex-forces' of their female initiates, and, unlike that of the Golden Dawn, it appears that their work was eminently practical.

A German iron tycoon named Karl Kellner is said to have visited India during the 1890's and to have made the acquaintance of an authentic Tantric Yogi, who initiated him into many of the secrets of that particular form of esoterism. Now Tantric Yoga is different from other forms of yoga in that sexual intercourse is used as a means for attaining Enlightenment, and upon his return to Germany, Kellner seems to have pursued Enlightenment with all due vigour. He formed a group in 1895 called the *Ordo Templi Orientis*, which admitted both men and women, and which taught Tantric sexual magic to its advanced students. Some of the most unlikley people joined Kellner's Order, including Rudolf Steiner, who became Austrian Chief of the OTO, Franz Hartmann, the eminent Theosophist, and Theodore Reuss, who succeeded Kellner as Outer Head of the Order. Publicly, the leaders of both the OTO and the GD recommended 'chastity' as a precondition for occult development, while in private they pursued a somewhat different course, and they were not the only ones.

In a recent book, Marion Meade notes with astonishment that 'at the age of fifty-four, in spite of two husbands, an indeterminate number of lovers, and a child' Madame Blavatsky 'solemnly insisted she was a virgin.'[33] She seems to have been very concerned with the question of sex, and insisted that members of her Esoteric Section give it up altogether. 'Black Magic', in her opinion, was connected in some manner with practising occultism while neglecting to practise chastity.

In The Key to Theosophy she alludes to certain 'physiological questions' which justify this position and which she refused to discuss. More important, though, was her feeling that no man can serve two masters, and that occultism was, in her words, 'a jealous mistress'. She considered 'practical Occultism' to be 'far too serious and dangerous a study for a man to take up, unless he is in the most deadly earnest', and as Lysistrata well knew, earnest doesn't get much deadlier than when one gives up sex. She is herself proof that sex and occult development are not incompatible, however, and that moreover, hypocrisy and occult development are not incompatible, either.

Yeats speaks of a disciple of hers who tried to practise chastity and who seems to have suffered from the sexual equivalent of the binge-purge syndrome. He was a 'young man', said Yeats, and he

filled [Madame Blavatsky] with exasperation, for she thought that his settled gloom came from his chastity. I had known him in Dublin where he had been accustomed to long periods of ascetism . . . with brief outbreaks of what he considered the devil. After an outbreak he would for a few hours dazzle the imagination of the members of the local Theosophical Society with poetical rhapsodies about harlots and street lamps, and then sink into weeks of melancholy.[34]

Another of her disciples, Mohini Chatterjee, was married, and yet nonetheless was able to make psychic contact with Mahatma Koot Hoomi. Upon his arrival in Paris, he seems to have dazzled the ladies, who imagined that he practised true Theosophical chastity, and at least one of them – an Englishwoman named Miss Leonard – set out to try to change all that.

According to her fellow Theosophists, she swore to seduce him. She pursued him into his bedroom, and when that did not produce the desired result, she stripped to the waist in a public park. Eventually, she got her man, and of course all this got back to H. P. Blavatsky, who, according to Meade, 'responded with a mixture of jealousy and repugnance.' Yet 'noticeable' in her letters, says Meade, 'is Helena's own thrill at imagining a "nut-meg Hindu" in the arms of a fair-skinned "too-erotic spinster." Her sexuality, rigidly repressed for a decade, could not help but reveal itself.'[35]

It revealed itself again when Mabel Collins, author of *Light on the Path* and editor of *Lucifer*, became 'plainly entangled with two young men, who were expected to grow into ascetic sages.' Yeats described her as 'a handsome, clever woman of the world, who seemed certainly very much out of place, penitent though she thought herself.' Her indiscretion caused 'much scandal and gossip', Yeats says, and she was dressed down soundly by Madame Blavatsky, who told her, 'I cannot permit you more than one.'[36] Meade considers this story 'probably apocryphal since H.P.B. was as adamantly anti-sex as she was anti-Mabel', but chastity was restored all round.[37] In a letter written later on, Koot Hoomi wrote that Blavatsky had 'deprived [Mabel] of a toy' and that she could be expected to retaliate, which she did, shortly afterwards.[38] Nobody who has read her *Caves and Jungles of Hindustan* can help noticing the relish with which Blavatsky recalled watching naked boys wandering around India. With those facts in mind, it is hard to take her pronouncements about chastity very seriously.

A more serious matter is the contention of sex-starved medieval priests that astral sex is dangerous. Here we would seem to be getting into questions of fact, and not opinion, and the stories reported by the priests tended to be, as one modern commentator put it, 'fraught with horror'.[39] It is too much to expect of frail human nature that a celibate would be sympathetic to the sexual activities of others, and during the Middle Ages, at least, celibate priests equated sex with sin and chastity with goodness. Astral sex to them must therefore be sex with a devil, and it is notable that an erotic ghost was never referred to as an incubus or a succuba, but as an 'incubus *devil*' or a 'succuba *devil*'. I mention this just to put their opinion on record, although I must say that I disagree with it. More objective reporters seem to have more positive things to say.

The following story appeared in volume six of the *Proceedings of the Society for Psychic Research*, and is typical of more modern accounts.

On 3 October, 1863, I sailed from Liverpool for New York. On the evening of the second day out a severe storm began, which lasted for nine days. Upon the night following the eighth day of the storm, I dreamed that I saw my wife, whom I had left in the United States, come to the door of my state-room, clad in her night-dress. At the door, she seemed to discover that I was not the only occupant of the room, hesitated a little, then advanced to my side, stooped down and kissed me, and after gently caressing me for a few moments, quietly withdrew. Upon waking I was surprised to see my fellow-passenger, whose berth was above mine, but not directly over it, leaning upon his elbow and looking fixedly at me. 'You're a pretty fellow', said he at length, 'to have a lady come and visit you in this way.' I pressed him for an explanation, which he at first declined to give. At length he related what he had seen while wide awake, lying in his berth. It corresponded exactly with my dream. The day after landing, almost [my wife's] first question when we were alone together was, 'Did you receive a visit from me a week ago Tuesday?' On the same night when the storm had just begun to abate, she had lain awake for a long time thinking of me, and about four o'clock in the morning it seemed to her that she went out to seek me. Crossing the wide and stormy sea, she came at length to a low, black steamship, whose side she went up, and then descending into the cabin, passed through it to the stern until she came to my state-room. 'Tell me', she said, 'do they ever have state-rooms like the one I saw, where the upper berth extends further back than the lower one? A man was in the upper berth, looking right at me, and for a moment I was afraid to go in. But soon I went up to the side of your berth, bent down, and kissed you, and embraced you, and then went away.'[40]

The fact that she 'hesitated' upon seeing that her husband was not alone suggests that she might have had something more than just a kiss in mind. In *The Llewellyn Practical Guide to Astral Projection*, Melita Denning and Osborne Phillips point out that something more would indeed have been possible, and moreover, that the woman in this situation has a decided advantage.[41]

The second possibility, in which *both* partners are 'exteriorized' at the time of the incident, is more rare than the incubus or succuba phenomenon, because each partner 'finds' the other on the astral plane, rather than deliberately projecting to the other's presence. Robert Monroe, who includes a chapter on astral sex in his *Journeys Out of the Body*, describes the experience as what two oppositely charged electrodes would 'feel' if they had consciousness. He says

They would 'need' to come together. There is no barrier that can restrain it. The need increases progressively with nearness. At a given point of nearness, the need is compelling. Very close, it is all-encompassing. Beyond a given point of nearness, the attraction-need exerts tremendous pull, and the two unlikes rush together and envelope one another. In an immediate moment, there is a mind (soul?) shaking interflow of electrons, one to the other, unbalanced charges become equalized, peaceful contented balance is restored, and each is revitalized. All this happens in an instant, yet an eternity passes by. Afterward, there is calm and serene separation.[42]

Compared to the astral experience, he says, physical sex is a mere shadow.

5. The Kama Loca

As I pointed out in the last chapter, there are many people who believe that sex is evil, and that particularly *astral* sex must be the work of 'evil demons', trying to ensnare the faithful. Although it is never stated in so many words, the implied basis of this view is that *inequality* is evil, and that, by extension, jealousy constitutes some kind of moral imperative. This theory has been widely accepted historically, and although I do not agree with it, one point made by such people may have some merit; namely, that the over-eager among us where sex is concerned may be 'held down' to the more sensuous levels of the astral plane. Such a person remains completely conscious of earthly conditions and happenings, rather than disappearing off into some other realm of existence. This would make it difficult for the astral projector to project into more rarefied levels, and it would also tend to make the spirit of a recently deceased person 'earthbound'. The Tibetans call these spirits *Pretas*, which means 'hungry ghosts', or 'unhappy ghosts', and they consider the earthbound state little better than consignment to the Hell-worlds themselves.

Milton, who was certainly no friend of sex, makes this point very emphatically in his *Comus*, where he says that

When lust,
By unchaste looks, loose gestures, and foul talk,
But most by lewd and lavish act of sin,
Lets in defilement to the inward parts.
The soul grows clotted by contagion,
Imbodies, and imbrues, until she quite lose
The divine property of her first being.
Such are those thick and gloomy shadows damp
Oft seen in charnel vaults and sepulchres,

Lingering, and sitting by a new-made grave
As loath to leave the body that it lov'd,
And linked itself by carnal sensuality
To a degenerate and degraded state.[1]

Whew! the gentleman doth protest too much. There is hardly any
doubt that Milton was thinking of Plato's *Phaedo* when he wrote this,
especially the part where Socrates tells Cebes about souls 'prowling
about tombs and sepulcres, in the neighbourhood of which, as they tell
us, are seen certain ghostly apparitions of souls which have not departed
pure, but are cloyed with sight and [are] therefore visible.'[2] Socrates did
not see these souls as being punished specifically for their interest in sex,
though. He thought they were insufficiently *intellectual*. He says that this
happens to the soul who is 'in love with and fascinated by the body, and
by the desires and pleasures of the body, until she is led to believe that
the truth exists only in bodily form, which a man may touch and see and
taste and use for the purpose of his lusts. She is engrossed by the
corporeal.' After death, 'she is afraid of the invisible, and of the world
below', hence clings to the world she knows.[3]

Conan Doyle says the 'earth-bound' 'are held on or near the surface
of this world by the grossness of their nature or by the intensity of their
worldly interests. So coarse may be the texture of their other-worldly
form, that they may even bring themselves within the cognisance of
those who have no special gift of clairvoyance.' He says that this is the
explanation of 'ghosts, spectres, apparitions, and hauntings', and that
'these people have not even commenced their spiritual life either for
good or evil. It is only when the strong earth ties are broken that the new
existence begins.'[4]

For the traveller on the astral plane, this most sensuous level will be
the first realm contacted. Most Western students of projection in fact
never advance beyond it. Hence, it will be worth our while to take a
closer look at it.

A few centuries ago, it was commonly believed that spirits walked to
guard some earthly possession that they treasured too greatly in life.
Thus, in *Hamlet*, Shakespeare's character addresses a ghost in the
following words:

If thou hast uphoarded in thy life
Extorted treasure in the womb of earth,
For which, they say, you spirits oft walk in death,
Speak of it. Stay, and speak.

Not everyone was wealthy enough to have an 'extorted treasure in the womb of earth', though, and some spirits were believed to walk for other reasons.

Plutarch says,

> They tell of Pausanias that when he was in Byzantium, he solicited a young lady of noble family, whose name was Cleonice, to debauch her. Her parents, dreading this cruelty, were forced to consent, and so abandoned their daughter to his wishes. The daughter asked the servants outside the chamber to put out all the lights, so that approaching silently and in the dark toward his bed, she stumbled upon a lamp, which she overturned. Pausanias, who had fallen asleep, was awakened and startled by the noise, and thought an assassin had taken that dead time of night to murder him. Hastily snatching up his poniard, he struck the girl, who fell by the blow and died. After this he was continually haunted by her, and saw her visiting him in sleep, and addressing him with these angry words:
>
> 'Come, meet thy doom
> By pride are men undone'
>
> Continuing, it is said, to be disturbed by the apparition, he fled to the oracle of the dead at Heraclea, where he raised the ghost of Cleonice, and pleaded to be reconciled with her. She appeared to him, and answered, that as soon as he should come to Sparta, he would be freed.[5]

It would appear that the prophecy was 'obscurely' fulfilled, as Dryden has it, for shortly after Pausanias arrived at Sparta he died, and the ghost of Cleonice walked no more.

In his *Life of Cimon*, Plutarch tells a similar tale about a bandit named Damon, who 'ravaged the country all about' Chaeronea and who greatly irritated the good people of the city. They were careful not to let him know how they felt, but, 'by messages and decrees in appearance favourable enticed him into the city.' Once there, 'as he was anointing himself in the vapour baths, they set upon him and killed him,' but they did not kill his spirit, which, being coarse, clung to the earth plane. As a result, 'for a long while after, apparitions were seen, and groans were heard in that place, so they ordered the gates of the baths to be sealed up, and even to this day those who live in the neighbourhood believe they sometimes see spectres, and hear alarming sounds.[6]

In some cases, ghosts are said to have walked because they were not properly buried. One suspects that this belief is a major reason why such elaborate funeral ceremonies are held for the dead.

In the *Letters* of Pliny the Younger, we read of a 'goodly and very large house' in Athens which suffered from 'evil repute' and was 'counted as unfortunate and unlucky' for just such a reason.

For about midnight there was heard the noise of iron, and if one marked it well, the rattling of chains, far off at first, and so, nearer and nearer. Shortly there appeared an image or shape, as it were an old man, lean and loathsome to behold, with a long beard and staring hair. On his legs he had fetters, and in his hands carried chains which he always rattled together. Those that inhabited the house, by reason of their fear, watched many heavy and pitiful nights. And after their watching followed sickness, and soon after, as fear increased, ensued death. For in the daytime also, albeit the image were departed, yet the remembrance thereof was ever before their eyes, so that their fear was longer than they had cause to fear.

Upon this the house stood solitary and deserted, entirely left unto the monster who inhabited it, yet was it proclaimed to be sold, if happily any man, who was ignorant of this great mischief, would either buy or hire it. Athenodorus chanced to come to Athens and read the writing on the door. When he learned the price he was astonished at how cheap it was. Inquiring further, he understood the whole matter, and notwithstanding anything that he heard, he hired the house.

When night came, he commanded his servants to make his bed in the utter part of the house. He took his writing tables, his writing wire, and a candle, and sent all his servants into the inner part of the house. He then set about to write, lest, his mind being unoccupied, he should imagine that he heard strange things, and breed vain fears. In the beginning of the night there was silence, but not long after the iron began to ring, and the chains to move. He would not look up or cease his writing, but hardened his heart and stopped his ears. Then the noise increased and drew near, and seemed sometimes to be outside the porch, sometimes within. Athenodorus looked back and saw the spectre, standing still and beckoning with its finger as though summoning him. The philosopher on the other side signified with his hand that he should stay a while, and went back to his writing. As he sat, the ghost shook its chains over his head. Looking around, he saw it beckoning again, as before. And so rising up without delay, taking his candle in his hand, he followed. The image went before with a stately pace, as if he were heavily laden with chains. After he had turned aside into the court of the house, he suddenly vanished, leaving his walking mate alone.

Athenodorus gathered herbs and leaves over the place where the ghost had disappeared, then went to the rulers of the city the following day to urge that the spot be dug up. It was done, and bones were found, wrapped and tied in chains. The bones were gathered together and buried solemnly, and the house was ever after cleared of all such ghosts.[7]

Herodotus tells a similar tale of the tyrant Periander,

One day he stripped all the women of Corinth stark naked, for the sake of his own wife, Melissa. He had sent messengers to Thesprotia to consult the oracle of the dead upon the [River] Acheron concerning a pledge which had been given into his charge by a stranger, and Melissa appeared, but refused to speak or tell where the pledge was. "She was chill," she said, 'having no clothes. The garments buried with her were of no use, since they had not been burnt.' When this message was brought him, Periander straightaway made proclamation, that all the wives of the Corinthians should go forth to the temple of Hera. The women appareled themselves in their bravest, and went forth, as if to a festival. Then, with the help of his guards, whom he had placed for the purpose, he stripped them one and all, making no difference between the free women and the slaves, and, taking their clothes to a pit, he called on the name of Melissa, and burned the whole heap. This done, he sent a second time to the oracle, and Melissa's ghost told him where he would find the stranger's pledge.[8]

Now, in many cases what was desired was not to *evoke* a ghost, but to lay one to rest. Every tribe has a taboo against the living mingling socially with the dead, and it is for that reason that cemeteries are carefully segregated from communities. Primitive peoples, in both the East and West, believe it worthwhile to leave offerings of food for the dead, because even though they cannot eat the physical food itself, the odours are supposed to be nourishing to spirits. This is supposed to be the origin of the Feasts on the Night of All Souls. One of the very strangest of these stories concerns a brave English knight named William Laudun.

Laudun flourished in the twelfth century, but not happily, because a Welsh sorcerer who died in his town refused to stay buried. 'Four nights [after his death] he came back,' said the knight, and 'he *keeps* coming every night, calling by name certain of his former neighbours.' After having this weird experience they 'instantly fall sick and die within three days.' Now he said that 'but few of them [were] left' by the time he decided to do something about this, and one suspects from that that the 'ghost' would have laid *itself* to rest shortly. But Sir William was himself one of the wizard's neighbours, and waiting was for him out of the question. He visited a local bishop and asked what to do.

'The bishop suggested that the evil angel of this dead villain had perhaps reanimated his body, and advised the knight to have it dug up and beheaded, and then buried again after the grave had been copiously sprinkled with holy water', says Kittredge. 'All this proved of no avail, and at length the name of Sir William himself was called. Seizing his sword, he pursued the demonic corpse to the churchyard, and, just as it was sinking into the grave, cleft its head to the neck. There was no further trouble.'[9]

Lafcadio Hearn tells an interesting tale in his book, *Gleanings in Buddha-Fields*, which he translated from a Japanese book, and which gives a vivid picture of life in *Kama-Loca* from the point of view of one who lived it.

The story is that of a young Japanese boy, named Katsugoro, who was convinced that he had lived before as the son of Kyubei San of Hodokubo, and that he had died at the age of six, a victim of smallpox. At first, the child entrusted this strange story only to his sister, but his grandmother, hearing the children talking among themselves one day, became curious about it, and drew it out of him. It is particularly interesting, because it comes from a country in the Far East, and yet verifies in many details the reports of witnesses from the Western world.

Until I was four years old I used to remember everything, but since then I have become more and more forgetful. And now I forget many, many things. But I still remember that I died of smallpox. I remember that I was put into a jar. I remember that I was buried on a hill. There was a hole made in the ground, and the people let the jar drop into the hole. It fell *pon!* I remember that sound well. Then, somehow, I returned to the house, and I stopped on my own pillow there. In a short time some old man – looking like my grandfather – came and took me away. I do not know who or what he was. As I walked I went through empty air as if flying. I remember that it was neither night nor day as we went. It was always like sunset-time. I did not feel either warm or cold or hungry. We went very far, I think, but still I could hear always, faintly, the voices of people talking at home, and the sound of the *Nembutsu* being said for me. I remember also that when the people at home set offerings of hot *botamochi* before the household shrine, I inhaled the vapour of the offerings. Never forget to offer warm food to the honourable dead . . . I am sure it is very good to do these things . . . After that, I only remember that the old man led me by some roundabout way to this place – I remember we passed the road beyond the village. Then we came here, and he pointed to this house and said to me, 'Now you must be reborn, for it is three years since you died. The person who will become your grandmother is very kind, so it will be well for you to be conceived and born there.' After saying this, the old man went away. I remained a little time under the kaki-tree before the entrance of this house. Then I was going to enter when I heard talking inside. Someone said that because father was now earning so little, mother would have to go to service in Yedo. I thought, 'I will not go into that house', and I stopped three days in the garden. On the third day it was decided that, after all, mother would not have to go to Yedo. The same night I passed into the house through a knothole in the sliding shutters, and after that I stayed for three days in the kitchen. Then I entered mother's honourable womb . . . I remember that I was born without any pain at all.

Katsugoro's grandmother, having heard all this, went with the boy to the house where he claimed to have spent his previous incarnation, to see if such a person as he claimed to have been had ever lived there. When he recognized the house, Katsugoro 'ran in, without waiting for his grandmother. Tsuya followed him, and asked . . . whether there had ever been a son called Tozo born in that house. "Yes," was the answer, *"but that boy died thirteen years ago, when he was six years old."*[10]

Another such story comes from a man who believed that he had been killed in his last life by bandits. He had been an avaricious man in life, and in death passed the period between incarnations as a *Preta*.

His recollections were confused and obscure. The Buddhist priest who interviewed him says

It seemed to him that for a long time he wandered about the scene of his former life, conscious only of a sense of loss and profound unhappiness. In this condition he appeared to have no judgement of the passage of time and was unable to say whether it lasted for days or centuries. His sense of personal identity, too, was very feeble, his thoughts revolving entirely around the events just prior to his death, and the memory of his lost treasure.

Eventually 'he became aware of living beings, and felt an attraction toward a certain young woman.' He followed her about, and in some manner he did not completely understand, was reborn as her child.[11]

Now that seems considerably more pleasant than the 'thirty-six orders of hideous misery' described by Lafcadio Hearn. The Buddhists see the *Preta*-realm as a very undesirable place to spend the period between lifetimes, but from what we can gather from interviews with people who believe themselves to have been former *Pretas*, it seems rather neutral.

In *The Search For Bridey Murphy*, Morey Bernstein paints a rather vivid picture of life as a *Preta*, based on the recollections of Ruth Simmons while under hypnotic trance. She says that she found herself in a world with no day and no night – only twilight, just as Katsugoro and others have reported. She passed her time by watching the living and just 'willing' herself from place to place.[12] Nonetheless, she considered this sort of 'life' to be inferior to life on earth. 'It wasn't full enough', she said. 'It wasn't . . . just couldn't do all the things . . . couldn't accomplish anything and . . . couldn't talk to anybody very long. They'd go away . . . didn't stay very long.'[13] When it was time for her to be reborn, she was given the news by some women, unlike Katsugoro, who was told by a man.[14] Perhaps the messenger is always of the same sex as the ghost – could it be?

Madame Blavatsky, who had so much to say about these matters, suggests that most of the *Pretas* are not really ghosts at all, but astral corpses, which are discarded by the soul as it rises from plane to plane. This idea comes from the writings of Eliphas Levi, although similar beliefs are held in the Far East.

In *The Mysteries of Magic*, Eliphas explains that

nothing can enter Heaven save that which comes from Heaven. The divine spirit [therefore] must ultimately return alone into the Empyrean, and thus two corpses are left by it in the earth and in the atmosphere, the one terrestrial and elementary, the other aerial and sidereal – the one already inert, the other still animated by the universal movement of the soul which created it, but destined to die gradually, being absorbed by the astral energies which produced it.[15]

This is the Qabalistic notion of 'shells' – the astral corpse being called a 'shell' because, like the decaying physical body, although it reminds one of its owner, the vital part of the owner – the soul – is not there. In the 'later Kabbalah', as Waite calls it, this notion of shells is connected with some very weird ideas indeed. The shells are said to inhabit the worlds beneath Assiah, the world of the Qlippoth, or Qabalistic demons.[16]

Now it is interesting that in Chinese folklore, where these 'shells' are called *houen*, we find the very same idea. According to one early interpreter of Chinese thinking, a French missionary who published a book about the Chinese in the eighteenth century,

the *houen* hold the middle between man and the brute and participate of the faculties of both. They have all the vices of man and every dangerous instinct of the animal. Sentenced to ascend no higher than our atmosphere, they congregate around the tombs and in the vicinity of mines, swamps, sinks, and slaughterhouses – everywhere wherein rottenness and decay are found. The emnanations of the latter are their favourite food, and it is with the help of those elements and atoms, and of the vapours from corpses, that they form for themselves terrible and fantastic bodies with which to deceive and frighten men.[17]

In *Isis Unveiled*, Madame Blavatsky refers to 'the disembodied souls of the depraved' as 'elementary spirits'.

Eliphas Levi and some other Kabalists [sic] make no distinction between elementary spirits who have been men, and those beings which people the elements and are the blind forces of nature. Once divorced from their bodies, these souls of purely materialistic persons are irresistibly attracted to the earth, where they live a temporary and finite life amid elements congenial to their gross natures. From having never, during their natural lives, cultivated their spirituality, but subordinated it to the material and gross, they are now unfitted for the lofty career of the pure, disembodied being, for whom the atmosphere of earth is stifling and mephitic, and whose attractions are all away from it.[18]

Although she calls the elementaries 'souls', she says that they are 'separated from their divine spirits' and that 'after a more or less prolonged period of time these material souls will begin to disintegrate, and finally, like a column of mist, be dissolved, atom by atom, in the surrounding elements.'[19] It is clear that she accepted this Buddhist and Chinese conception then, and in her later writings she gives a very sophisticated interpretation of this phenomenon indeed.

When man dies, the lower three principles leave him forever, and then his four [remaining] principles find themselves in *Kama-Loca*. The latter is an astral locality, the *limbus* of scholastic theology, the *Hades* of the ancients, and, strictly speaking, a *locality* only in a relative sense. It has neither a definite area nor boundary, but is beyond our sensuous perceptions. It is there that all the astral *eidolons* of the beings that have lived, animals included, await their *second death*. For the animals it comes with the disintegration and the entire fading out of their astral particles to the last. For the human *eidolon* it begins when the [higher] triad [of principles] begins to separate itself from its lower principles by falling into the Devachanic state. Then the *Kama-rupic* phantom collapses. It can think no more, even on the lowest animal plane. [It is] a true nonentity, however, only as to true reasoning powers. [It is] still an *entity*, however astral and fluidic, as shown in certain cases when, having been magnetically and unconsciously drawn toward a medium, it is revived for a time and lives in him by proxy, so to speak. In the medium's aura it lives a kind of vicarious life, and reasons and speaks either through the medium's brain or those of other persons present.[20]

She says that during the early part of her career, when she was a spiritualist, she

saw and watched these soulless creatures, which throve and preserved their semi-material shadows at the expense of the hundreds of visitors that came and went as well as of the mediums. At times I used to see one of such phantoms, quitting the medium's astral body, pouncing upon one of the sitters, expanding so as to envelop him or her entirely, and then slowly disappearing within the living body as though sucked in by its every pore. The spiritualist . . . wept and rejoiced around the medium, clothed in these empty materialised shadows. It was ghastly![21]

For certain psychomagnetic reasons, too long to be explained here, the shells of those spirits who loved us will not, with a few exceptions, approach us. They have no need of it, since they have us with them in Devachan, unless they were irretrievably wicked . . . . 'Shells', once separated from their higher principles, have nought in common with the latter. They are not drawn to their relatives and friends, but rather to those with whom their terrestrial, sensuous affinities are the strongest. Thus the shell of a drunkard will be drawn to one who is either a drunkard already or has a germ of this passion in him, in which case they will develop it by using his organs to satisfy their craving. One who died full of sexual passion for a still living partner will have its shell drawn to him or her, and so on.[22]

These simulacra of men and women are made up wholly of the terrestrial passions, vices, and worldly thoughts, of the residuum of the personality that was. For these are only such dregs that could not follow the liberated soul and spirit, and are left for a second death in the terrestrial atmosphere.[23]

It is difficult for even the traveller on the astral plane to 'follow the liberated soul and spirit', so lofty is the place where it is to go. But we can follow it in imagination, at least for now, and that will be where we meet next.

6. The World of Boundless Light

Robert Crookall, who has written several books about astral projection, believes there is a 'Hades belt' surrounding the earth through which one must pass on the way to what he calls 'Paradise conditions'. A projector emerges first into the 'Hades belt', which is called that because it resembles the 'Hades' of the Greeks, then crosses what appears to be a watery zone. This, he thinks is the reason the Greeks held that the souls of the dead had to cross the River Styx. This watery vision may take the form of a river, an ocean, a column of water vapour or a fog, but in each case the idea of *water* is present. If one makes it through this watery area, one finds oneself in a 'world of boundless light'.[1]

This idea is so logical that I suspect it is probably true. We do not know, of course, just why there would *be* such a 'Hades-belt', or why one would have a vision of water or mist upon leaving it, but we do know that people have these experiences. The only question is whether they have them necessarily in that order.

As for the 'world of boundless light' – and I am using a Buddhist term here – we have too many accounts from too many people for there to be any doubt that it exists.

One person who was regressed under hypnosis to the period between the end of his last lifetime and the beginning of this, said, 'I'm conscious of light everywhere. I seem to be wherever I think about. Souls are all around, and of course we can communicate. How? We just know!'[2]

A railroad engineer in Jacksonville, Florida, who had an accident while unloading a railroad car, says,

> I saw a medium-sized person standing at my right hand clothed in white with a bright countenance, beaming with intelligence. I knew what he wanted in an instant, although he put his hand on my shoulder and said, 'Come with me'. We moved upward, and a little

to the south-east, with the speed of lightning, as it were. I could see the hills, buildings, trees, and roads as we went up side by side until they vanished out of our sight. As we passed on, this glorious being that was with me told me he was going to show me the bright heavenly world. We soon came to a world of light and beauty, many thousand times larger than this earth, with at least four times as much light. The beauties of this place were beyond any human being to describe. I was seated by the tree of life on a square bunch of what appeared to be green velvet moss, about eighteen inches high. There I saw many thousand spirits clothed in white and singing the heavenly songs . . . . It was the sweetest song I have ever heard. I told my attendant that it was the first time I had ever been perfectly at rest in my life. They did not converse by sound, but each knew the other's thoughts at the instant, and conversation was carried on in that way, and also with me.

After viewing the wonderful beauties of the place for some time, and the thousands of spirits, robed in spotless white, passing through the air, for they did not confine themselves to the surface, but went every direction they pleased, I wanted to see my dear mother, two sisters, and a child of mine that had died some time before this. The request was granted at once, but I was not allowed to converse with them. They were standing in a row in front of me, and I looked at them and cooly estimated the distance we were apart at thirty feet, and wondered how these things could be. They seemed very much pleased to see me, and I shall never forget how they welcomed me when I first saw them, although no conversation passed. About this time my attendant told me we must go back. I wished to stay, but he told me my time had not come yet, but would in due time, and I should wait with patience. At this we started back, and were soon out of sight of that heavenly land. Then we came in sight of this world. I saw everything as it looked from a great height... till we came to the [railroad] car . . . and I found myself there in the body, and he vanished out of my sight.[3]

In Theosophical terminology, the 'world of boundless light' is known as *Devachan*, and it is conceived as a Karmic reward for good deeds done on earth, to be enjoyed before starting a new incarnation. Blavatsky says:

During every Devachanic period the Ego clothes itself with the reflection of the personality that was. The ideal efflorescence of all the eternal qualities, such as love and mercy, the love of the good, the true and beautiful, that ever spoke in the heart of the living personality, clung after death to the Ego, and therefore followed it to Devachan. It is an absolute oblivion of all that gave it pain or sorrow in the past incarnation, and even oblivion of the fact that such things as pain or sorrow exist at all. The *Devachanee* lives surrounded by everything it had aspired to in vain, and in the companionship of everyone it loves on earth.'[4]

Since 'everything it loves on earth' may still *be* on earth at the time the Devachanee begins to enjoy his reward, Devachan is conceived of as a sort of dream-state – illusory, like this world of *Maya* and deception, only more so, since the Devachanee creates it with his thoughts.

The fact that everyone describes the state in the same language, though, suggests to me that Devachan is a social reality. Now bear in mind that in the mystical sense *everything* is unreal, except for the Self. The fact that the Devachan-dweller may create positive conditions for himself with thought could only mean that thought is more creative in more rarefied spheres than in this. Moreover, according to Lafcadio Hearn, there are more than just one 'Devachan'.

The pilgrimage through death and birth must continue, for the majority of mankind at least, even after the attainment of the highest conditions possible upon this globe. The way rises from terrestrial conditions to other and superior worlds – passing first through the Six Heavens of Desire, thence through the Seventeen Heavens of Form, and lastly through the Four Heavens of Formlessness, beyond which lies Nirvana.

The requirements of physical life – the need of food, rest, and sexual relations – continue to be felt in the Heavens of Desire – which would seem to be higher physical worlds rather than what we commonly understand by the expression "heavens". Indeed, the conditions in some of them are such as might be supposed to exist in planets more favoured than our own – in larger spheres warmed by a more genial sun. And some Buddhist texts actually place them in remote constellations – declaring that the Path leads from star to star, from galaxy to galaxy, from universe to universe, up to the Limits of Existence.

In the first of the heavens of this zone, called the Heaven of the Four Kings, life lasts five times longer than life on earth according to number of years, and each year there is equal to fifty terrestrial years. but its inhabitants eat and drink, and marry and give in marriage, much after the fashion of mankind. In the succeeding heaven, the duration of life is doubled, while all other conditions are correspondingly improved. In the third heaven, where longevity is again doubled, the slightest touch may create life. In the fourth, or Heaven of Contentment, longevity is again increased. In the fifth, or Heaven of the Transmutation of Pleasure, strange new powers are gained. Subjective pleasures become changed at will into objective pleasures. Thoughts as well as wishes become creative forces, and even the act of seeing may cause conception and birth. In the six heaven, the powers obtained in the fifth heaven are further developed, and the subjective pleasures transmuted into objective can be presented to others, or shared with others – like material gifts. But the look of one instant – one glance of the eye – may generate a new Karma.

The Heavens of Desire are all heavens of sensuous life – heavens such as might answer to the dreams of artists and lovers and poets. But those who are able to traverse them without falling (and a fall, be it observed, is not difficult) pass into the supersensual Zone, first entering the Heavens of Luminous Observation of Existence and of Calm Meditation upon Existence. There are in number three – each higher than the preceding – and are named The Heaven of Sanctity, The Heaven of Higher Sanctity, and The Heaven of Great Sanctity. After these come the heavens called the Heavens of Luminous Observation of Non-Existence and of Calm Meditation upon Non-Existence. These are also three, and the names of them in order signify, Lesser Light, Light Unfathomable, and Light Making Sound, or, Light Sonorous. Here there is attained the highest degree of supersensuous joy possible to temporary conditions. Above are the states named the Heavens of the Meditation of the Abandonment of Joy. The names of these states in their ascending order are, Lesser Purity, Purity Unfathomable, and Purity Supreme. In them neither joy nor pain, nor forceful feeling of any kind exist. There is a mild negative pleasure only – the pleasure of Heavenly Equanmity. Higher than these heavens are the eight spheres of Calm Meditation upon the Abandonment of all Joy and Pleasure. They are called the Cloudless, Holiness-Manifest, Vast Results, Empty of Name, Void of Heat, Fair-Appearing, Vision-Perfecting, and The Limit of Form. Herein pleasure and pain, and name and form, pass utterly away. But there remain ideas and thoughts.

He who can pass through these supersensuous realms enters at once into the spheres of Formlessness. These are four. In the first state all sense of individuality is lost. Even the thought of name and form becomes extinct, and there survives only the idea of Infinite Space, or Emptiness. In the second state this idea of space vanishes, and its place is filled by the Idea of Infinite Reason. But this idea of reason is anthropomorphic. It is an illusion, and it fades out in the third state, which is called the State-of-Nothing-to-take-hold-of. Here is only the Idea of Infinite Nothingness. But even this condition has been reached by the aid of the action of the personal mind. This action ceases. Then the fourth state is reached – the state of 'neither-namelessness-nor-not-namelessness'. Something of personal mentality continues to float vaguely here – the very uttermost expiring vibration of Karma – the last vanishing haze of Being. It melts, and the immeasurable revelation comes. The dreaming Buddha, freed from the last ghostly bond of Self, rises at once into the 'infinite bliss' of Nirvana.[5]

Some Western commentators have described Nirvana as *annihilation*, but that is not quite correct, for a thing cannot be annihilated which never existed in the first place, and the Ego, according to Buddhist teaching, does not exist. It is what Alan Watts calls 'a conceptual hallucination'. And Nirvana, in Hearn's words, 'is no cessation, but an emancipation. It means only the passing of conditioned being into unconditioned being – the fading of all mental and physical phantoms into the light of Formless Omnipotence.'

7. Descent into Hell

In *La Science des esprits*, Eliphas Levi suggests that those who awaken from the sleep of death were not really buried prematurely at all, but were frightened by some vision of the other world. 'When a man falls into the last sleep, he is plunged into a sort of dream, before gaining consciousness on the other side of life. He sees, then, either in a beautiful vision, or in a terrible nightmare, the Paradise or Hell in which he believed during his mortal existence.'[1] Those who see Hell rather than Paradise, he suggests, take refuge in their decaying corpse, rather than face what they believe to be their fate.

If there is a Paradise, though, it would seem that a Hell would exist of necessity, because everything on the astral plane must have its opposite, and for a paradise to *be* a paradise, those who would make it less than heavenly would have to be excluded from it.

It is hard to imagine a Heaven with Argentine jailers, German Nazis, or medieval Inquisitors. Any society which has an identity *as a society* must exclude those who do not harmonize with its purposes and who would corrupt and defeat it if they had the chance. We cannot imagine the Masonic Lodge admitting anti-Masons or the Catholic Church admitting anti-Catholics. And it is impossible to imagine Heaven admitting anti-socials. If such persons have a share in life after death, there must be a separate place for them. There must be an astral slum.

It was not always called that. The Theosophists call it *Kama Loca*, or the 'lower astral plane'. Japanese Buddhists call it *Jigoku*, and Christians and Jews call it *Hell*. A recent Gallup poll showed that four out of five Englishmen reject the very notion that such a place exists. But exist it certainly does, if we believe those who have been there.

Some investigators who have studied the 'near death experience' say that all the experiences they heard were positive ones – visions of rolling meadows, beautiful cities, and relatives long gone. But in a recent book called *Beyond Death's Door*, Dr Maurice Rawlings challenges that. He says that some of the stories *he* has heard were most unpleasant indeed. One of them involved a middle-aged patient of his, a heart attack victim who 'died' several times in rapid succession in Dr Rawlings' presence. Each time the man died he was resuscitated, and each time he was resuscitated he cried out that he was in 'Hell'. Rawlings' efforts to save him eventually 'took' and the man made a complete recovery, denying later that he had ever had any unpleasant visions while 'dead'. But Rawlings was a shaken man. He believed that his patient really *had* been in Hell during those brief brushes with death, and that Hell as a place must really exist.

He began to interview other resuscitated patients, and he says that they reported *two* kinds of post-mortem visions and not just one. There are, of course, the visions of beautiful rolling meadows and cities of light, but there are others as well, 'inexpressibly horrible, frequently a dungeon or huge cave.'[2] These patients 'may enter a dark passage' just like the luckier ones, he says, 'but instead of emerging into bright surroundings they enter a dark, dim environment where they encounter grotesque people lurking in the shadows . . . . The horrors defy description and are difficult to recall.'[3] He likens Hell as described by his patients to 'a carnival's spook house' and he believes that these bad experiences are just as common as the good ones. They go unreported, perhaps because a trip to 'Hell' is not something one talks about, or perhaps because the patient cannot remember them. It is possible, Rawlings points out, that the experiences are so terrifying that the mind is unable to deal with them, and therefore represses and 'forgets' them shortly after they are over.[4]

In *At the Hour of Death*, Karlis Osis describes a survey that he conducted among physicians in the USA and in India to determine whether there was anything to these 'near death experiences' or whether they were just hallucinations. Like Rawlings, he concluded that the scenes described by dying men are real, and that the places they 'see' themselves going to are real places. And, like Rawlings, some of his patients saw threatening landscapes and were 'taken away' by visionary figures against their will. He does not think the percentage of such cases is as high as Dr Rawlings does, but he does place it at 17 per cent or so. They are therefore not rare.[5]

Raymond Moody found these kinds of experiences especially with people who had committed suicide. People commit suicide to escape earthly problems, of course, but instead of oblivion they find themselves completely conscious, and in a more gruesome place than the one they left. Moody says that 'in their disembodied state' the suicides he interviewed 'were unable to do anything about their problems, and yet they had to view the unfortunate consequence which had resulted from their acts.' One man says that he went 'to an awful place' and that he expected to be there for some time – a penalty as it were for 'breaking the rules'.[6] Still others report strange, gruesome obsessions.

'The thing was', said one suicide victim '[the problem] was still around, even when I was "dead". And it was like it was repeating itself, a rerun. I would go through it once and at the end I would think "Oh, I'm glad that's over". And then it would start all over again.'[7] In other cases, the obsession involves the act of suicide itself. In his visions the suicide 'dies' as the Wandering Jew wanders – endlessly.

'A suicide will repeat automatically the feelings of despair and fear which preceded his self-murder', says Annie Besant, 'and [will] go through the act and death struggle time after time with ghastly persistence.' Moreover, she says that this is the lot of all those who die violently, even if they do not initiate the process themselves.

> One man who had committed an assassination and had been executed for his crime was said to be living through the scenes of the murder and the subsequent events over and over again, ever repeating the diabolical act and going through the terrors of arrest and trial and execution. A woman who perished in the flames in a wild condition of terror and with frantic efforts to escape, created such a whirl of passion that, five days afterward, she was still struggling desperately, fancying herself still in the fire and wildly repulsing all efforts to sooth her.[3]

British novelist Charles Williams describes these experiences in some detail in *Descent Into Hell*, and since he was a member of the Hermetic Order of the Golden Dawn, and an experimenter in things psychic, Ithell Colquhoun believes his descriptions may have been based on actual observations on the astral plane. 'No one who had not explored the region which Theosophists call the Lower Astral Plane could have described, as he did, the purgatory of a suicide', she says. 'It is one of the most horrifying accounts anywhere.'[9] One of the characters in the book is a dead man, who hanged himself at a place called The Hill, and who haunted the spot, reliving the anguish which led up to his suicide, and trying again and again to kill himself, in a twilight world where the sun does not shine and the moon does not appear.

A more terrifying account than Williams', though, was left to us by Edgar Allen Poe, and was based on an actual experience of his. He suffered from cateleptic trances, similar to those induced voluntarily by the yogis, but unlike the yogis, Poe did not wish to enter these states, and his dreams were anything but pleasant.

Methought I was immersed in a cataleptic trance of more than usual duration and profundity, when suddenly there came an icy hand upon my forehead, and an impatient, gibbering voice whispered the word 'Arise' in my ear.

I sat erect. The darkness was total. I could not see the figure of him who had aroused me. I could call to mind neither the period at which I had fallen into the trance, nor the locality in which I then lay. While I remained motionless, and busied in endeavours to collect my thoughts, the cold hand grabbed me fiercely by the wrist, shaking it petulantly, while the gibbering voice said again,

'Arise! Did I not bid thee arise?'

'And who', I demanded, 'are thou?'

'I have no name in the Regions which I inhabit,' replied the voice, mournfully. 'I was mortal, but [now] am fiend. I was merciless, but [now] am pitiful. My teeth chatter as I speak, yet it is not with the chilliness of the night – of the night without end. But this hideousness is insufferable. How canst *thou* tranquilly sleep? I cannot rest for the cry of these great agonies. Come with me into the Outer Night, and let me unfold to thee the graves.'

I looked, and the unseen figure, which still grasped me by the wrist, had caused to be thrown open the graves of all mankind, and from each issued the faint phosphorescence of decay. Phantasies such as these extended their terrific influence far into my waking hours.[10]

Indeed! Less terrifying, but more detailed visions were left to us by Emmanuel Swedenborg, who believed, at least, that he had visited Hell in visions off and on for seventeen years.

In Swedenborg's visions the 'realms' were arranged hierarchically, with the Heavens above, the Hells below, and the 'World of Spirits' – which would correspond to the astral plane – in the middle. He says that in the World of Spirits 'there are hells under every mountain, hill, and rock, and under every plain and valley. The entire heaven and World of Spirits are, as it were, excavated beneath, and under them is a continuous hell.'[11] 'The Hells are not seen', he says, 'because they are closed up. Only the entrances, which are called gates, are seen when they are opened to let in other spirits.'[12] Even 'the gates and doors of the hells are visible only to those who are about to enter.'[13] Those gates which are beneath 'the mountains, hills, and rocks', he says, 'appear like holes and clefts in the rocks, some extended and wide, some straightened and narrow, and many of them rugged.'[14] As for those gates to be found beneath plains and valleys, 'some resemble those that are beneath the mountains, hills, and rocks; some resemble dens and caverns, some great chasms and whirlpools; some resemble bogs, and some standing water.'[15] At each gate 'a monster commonly appears that represents in a general way the forms of those within.'[16] 'When they are opened there bursts forth from them either something like the fire and smoke that is seen in the air from burning buildings, or like a flame without smoke, or like soot such as comes from a burning chimney, or like a mist and thick cloud.'[17] He says that 'a dense fire' comes from the gates of hells 'where the love of self prevails', and 'a flaming fire' from the gates of hells 'where the love of the world prevails.... When the hells are closed this fiery appearance is not seen, but in its place there is a kind of obscurity like a condensation of smoke, although the fire still rages within.' The hell-dwellers, though, are 'conscious of no burning' since 'the fire is only an appearance'. They feel 'only warmth, like that which they had felt when in the world' since they 'are as in their own atmosphere.'[18]

All the hells, 'when looked into, appear dark and dusky.'[19] 'When they are opened gloomy and seemingly sooty caverns and dens in rocks [are seen] extending inward and then downward, either obliquely or vertically, into an abyss, where there are many doors.'[20] Some of these looked like 'dens and caves of wild beasts in forests', whereas others resembled 'the hollow caverns and passages that are seen in mines, with caverns extending towards the lower regions.' Now from 'these caverns nauseous and fetid stenches exhale' which he compares with 'the odour from dung and excrement in the world.... In the worst hells [it is] like the odour of dead bodies.'[21] He says that 'evil spirits seek for [these smells] because they delight in them. For as every one in the world has been delighted with his own evil, so after death he is delighted with the stench to which his evil corresponds.'[22]

There are likewise hells beneath hells because in Swedenborg's view, the hells are threefold.

Some communicate with others by passages, and more by exhalations, the upper ones appearing to be in dense darkness... While the lower ones appear fiery.

Some hells present an appearance like the ruins of houses and cities after conflagrations, in which infernal spirits dwell and hide themselves. In the milder hells there is an appearance of rude huts, in some cases contiguous to the form of a city with lanes and streets, and within the houses are infernal spirits engaged in unceasing quarrels, enmities, fightings, and brutalities; while in the streets and lanes robberies and depredations are committed. In some of the hells there are nothing but brothels, disgusting to the sight and filled with every kind of filth and excrement. Again, there are dark forests, in which infernal spirits roam like wild beasts and where, too, there are underground dens into which those flee who are pursued by others. There are also deserts, where all is barren and sandy, and where in some places there are ragged rocks in which there are caverns, and in some places, huts. Into these desert places those are cast out from the hells who have suffered every extremity of punishment, especially those who in the world have been more cunning than others in undertaking and contriving intrigues and deceits. Such a life is their final lot.[23]

As for the Hell-dwellers themselves:

all spirits in the hells, when seen in any light of heaven, appear in the form of their evil.... It is impossible to describe how all these forms appear, for no one is like another, although there is a general likeness among those who are in the same evil.... In general, their faces are hideous, and void of life, like those of corpses. The faces of some are black, others fiery like torches, [still] others disfigured with pimples, warts, and ulcers. Some seem to have no face, but instead something hairy or bony, and with some only the teeth are seen. Their bodies are monstrous, and their speech is like the speech of anger or of hatred, or of revenge . . . But it must be understood that this is the way infernal spirits appear in the light of heaven, while among themselves they appear as men.[24]

As soon as any ray of light from heaven is let in, their human forms appear changed into monstrous forms... For in the light of heaven everything appears as it is. For this reason they shun the light of heaven and cast themselves down into their own light, which is like that of lighted coals, and in some cases like that from burning sulphur.[25]

Now in some respects, Swedenborg's conception of Hell agrees precisely with that in *The Tibetan Book of the Dead*, a book he could not have read. He says, for example, that 'if a man is in evil, he is tied to Hell, and in respect to his spirit is actually there, and after death desires nothing so much as to be where his evil is. Consequently, it is man who casts himself into Hell after death.'[26] In *The Tibetan Book of the Dead* we are told that the wanderer in the *Bardo* will see a dull, smoke-coloured light, and that he will find it pleasant, and will wish to move towards it. There are other similarities as well. Swedenborg also agrees on several points with the descriptions left to us by Plutarch, a writer he *could* have read. In one passage, he says that 'those who enter from a burning love of evil appear to be cast headlong, with the head downwards and the feet upwards.'[27] This could have come right out of Plutarch's *De Sera Numina Vindicti* (and may have), but Swedenborg said that he *saw* this done to 'one of the most deceitful' of those who 'have been inwardly wicked while maintaining an outward appearance of goodness'.[28]

Now if Swedenborg's visions resemble the visions described by Plutarch as well as the Buddhist conceptions in *The Tibetan Book of the Dead*, we would expect to find similarities also between the Buddhist conceptions and Plutarch's visions – and we do. The similarities here are more striking, though, and there is a different focus. Whereas Swedenborg's Hell is merely depressing, Plutarch's Hell is genuinely terrifying – and so is the Hell of the Buddhists.

Trungpa says of the Buddhist Hell-dweller that 'he finds himself walking through gigantic fields of red-hot iron, or being chained and marked with black lines and cut apart, or roasting in hot iron cubicles, or boiling in large cauldrons.' He makes it clear that these are hallucinations, and he says that they 'are generated from an environment of claustrophobia and aggression. There is a feeling of being trapped in a small space with no air to breathe and no room in which to move about. Trapped as he is, the [Hell-dweller] not only tries to destroy the walls of his claustrophobic prison; he even attempts to kill himself.' He cannot die, of course. He has already *done* that, and the more he struggles, 'the more solid and oppressive [the walls of his prison] become . . . . It is by withdrawing from them that they are mastered, for then they disappear.'[29]

Now the Hell-worlds are not inaccessible to the traveller on the astral plane. In *Journeys Out of the Body*, Robert Monroe describes some out-of-the-body experiences that he believes may have been a trip to the outer fringes of that not-so-nice region. But is it a place you would *want* to visit? Let me answer that question with a story from Eliphas Levi's *La Clef des Grands Mystères*.

He says he was told the story *'comme certaine'*, but that he would not altogether guarantee its authenticity.

Certain persons who doubted religion and magnetism at the same time, those *incredules* who are ready for all the superstitions and all the fanaticisms, decided to pay a poor girl in silver to submit to their experiments. She was of a nervous, impressionable nature, fatigued, moreover, by the excesses of a more than irregular life, and already disgusted with existence. She is put to sleep, and commanded to see; she weeps and argues. They speak to her of God . . . she trembles in every limb.

– 'No', she says, 'No, he fills me with dread. I will not look at him.'
– 'Look. I want you to.'
She opens her eyes; her pupils are dilated; she is terrified.
– 'What do you see?'
– 'I do not know how to say . . . Oh! Mercy, mercy, awaken me!'
– 'No, look and say what you see.'
– 'I see a black night in which whirling flashes surround two great eyes which are rolling around. From these eyes shoot rays which roll in spirals and which fill all space. Oh! It harms me! Awaken me!'
– 'No, look.'
– 'Where would you have me look now?'
– 'Look into Paradise.'
– 'No, I may not mount there; the great night takes me back and causes me to fall.'
– 'Very well, look into Hell.'
At this, the somnambulist shook convulsively.
– 'No! No!, she cried, sobbing, 'I will not. I would have vertigo. I would fall. Oh! Hold me back! Hold me back!'
– 'No, descend.'
– 'Where would you have me descend?'
– 'Into Hell.'
– 'But it is horrible! No, no, I will not go there.'

– 'Go.'
– 'Mercy!'
– 'Go there, I want you to.'
The features of the somnambulist became terrible to see. Her hair stood erect on her head. Her eyes, too widely opened, showed only the white. Her breast heaved, and let escape a sort of rattle.
– 'Go there, I want you to', repeated the magnetizer.
– 'I am there', said the unfortunate between her teeth, and fell exhausted. Then, she responded no more. Her inert head reclined on her shoulder. Her arms hung long beside her body. She was approached. She was touched. An effort was made too late to awaken her. The crime was accomplished. The girl was dead . . .

Levi says that 'the authors of this sacrilegious experiment . . . were not pursued' because of 'public incredulity in matters of magnetism . . . . The authorities wrote out a death certificate, and it was attributed to the rupture of an aneurism. The body carried moreover no sign of violence. It was interred, and everything had been said.'[30]

8. How to Get There

Having discussed the various realms of the astral plane, we have now to say something about how to *get* there. I must say at the first that I would discourage anyone from attempting suspended animation, unless he or she has someone in attendance to give medical attention if needed. The Indian government outlawed the practice of burial alive in 1955, because so many *sadhus* were being eaten alive by white ants while their bodies lay in *samadhi*. But even if you do not have yourself buried, there are dangers.

At least one man that I know of has died while attempting suspended animation – a fellow in New Jersey whose body was discovered in 1972. The cause of death was ascertained from a sort of diary that he kept, describing his experiments, and the case was listed in the newspapers as the strangest death in American medical history. There is hardly any point in trying to conceal the *modus operandi*, however, because anyone familiar with *pranayama* and self-hypnosis can figure it out easily enough, I know. Until I read about the aforementioned death, I was doing it myself.

Edgar Allen Poe, who suffered attacks of a strange disease known as catalepsy, has left us some of the most ingenious descriptions of suspended animation, although there are of course some differences if one enters the state voluntarily.

He says that he would sink,

little by little, into a condition of semi-syncope, or half swoon, and in this condition without pain, without ability to stir, or, strictly speaking, to think, but with a dull, lethargic consciousness of life and the presence of those who surrounded my bed. At other times I was quickly and impetuously smitten. I grew sick, and numb, and chilly, and dizzy, and so fell prostrate at once. Then for weeks all was void and silent, and Nothing became the universe. Total annihilation could be no more. From these latter attacks I awoke, however, with a gradation slow in proportion to the suddenness of the seizure. Just as the day dawns to the friendless and houseless beggar who roams the streets throughout the long desolate winter night – just so tardily – just so wearily – just so cheerily came back the light of the Soul to me.

On one occasion, he says,

I found myself emerging from total unconsciousness into the first feeble and indefinite sense of existence. Slowly – with a tortoise gradation – approached the faint grey dawn of the psychal day. A torpid uneasiness. An apathetic endurance of dull pain. No care – no hope – no effort. Then, after a long interval, a ringing in the ears. After a lapse still longer, a pricking or tingling sensation in the extremities. Then a seemingly eternal period of pleasurable quiescence, during which the awakening feelings are struggling into thought. Then a brief re-sinking into nonentity. Then a sudden recovery. At length the slight quivering of an eyelid, and immediately thereupon, an electric shock or terror, deadly and indefinite, which sends the blood in torrents from the temples to the heart. And now the first positive effort to think. And now the first endeavour to remember. And now a partial and evanescent success . . .

When the state is induced voluntarily, it comes slowly, just as Poe described, and is in fact approached gradually over a period of months, one session at a time. The only difference is, that in *voluntary* suspended animation the experimenter never loses consciousness. One is aware of entering a sleep almost as deep as death itself – at least where the body is concerned – yet the mind is totally awake, completely active. The soul, or the astral body, if you will, begins to separate itself from the body for brief periods of time, and, if the experiment is carried to its logical conclusion, it leaves as it would in death, for finer and more nebulous realms. The only problem is getting back.

There is a tendency to panic during these experiments, and if they have reached an advanced state, the experimenter quickly finds there is *reason* for panic. He will try to get up out of the chair he is sitting in; his muscles will not obey him. His eyes will not open. His heartbeat cannot be felt. He has as it were re-entered a corpse. Gradually, his vital processes begin to start up again, and his muscles, oxygen-starved, go into violent convulsions. It is *extremely* important to maintain rigid self-control during this phase, since these convulsions can be dangerous. They are, in any event, extraordinarily painful.

That does not leave us forever earthbound, however, because there are ways of achieving astral projection without going through any such extreme procedure. I only recommend suspended animation in any case to those who are very old and who have had their fill of life. It is an interesting experiment, to be sure, but irresponsible for the young.

A preferred procedure is what we might call the projection of visualized images. It is a variation on the techniques used by crystal gazers to develop clairvoyance, and works extremely well for one with sufficient determination to stick with it.

What you must do is sit in a comfortable chair, facing an unadorned wall, in front of which you will have placed some object just long enough to form a good mental image of it, and close your eyes, with the mental determination that you will not thereby lose sight of the object. Now this sounds strange, but all it means is that, while your eyes are closed, you will replace the sight of the scene you have just observed with a perfect visualization of the same scene. In other words, you will try to 'see' the same thing with your eyes either opened or closed.

Now some people will immediately object that it is *impossible* to see with one's eyes closed, and according to conventional wisdom, this is true. However, it is also 'impossible', according to that same conventional wisdom, to do astral projection. *Everything* we are trying to do here is unconventional, yet it can be done, and it is by *trying* to do it repeatedly that the necessary abilities are cultivated. All we are doing by performing the experiment in this way is structuring our efforts, and yet this very structuring is crucial to eventual success.

Some people like to combine this exercise with long periods of mantra meditation. Others like to do it in front of a clock. If they can 'see' the correct time, even though they have had their eyes closed for a good while, it is instant proof of success. Your first successes will come spontaneously, while you are perhaps meditating, or dropping off to sleep. You may sit down and close your eyes with no thought of astral projection, yet find yourself 'stepping out' for a brief trip across the room, or perhaps into the street. When you wake up in the morning, you may find that you can 'see' your bedroom dimly with your eyes closed. All these things are signs of success, and that brings me to the next point.

Success in astral projection seems to unbalance some people. After all, people are not 'supposed' to be able to waltz out of their bodies and stroll in the invisible to distant places. And there is a feeling in most of us that what we are not supposedly *able* to do we *should* not do. This is the herd instinct asserting itself. Without it, society as we know it would be impossible. But in some people it produces panic.

I suspect that one has to be an incorrigible non-conformist to do astral projection successfully, and if you find after your first few 'trips' that you *still* panic, you may want to discontinue your experiments. There are therapists who treat phobias, but the phobia of astral projection is not recognized by most of them. You are pretty much on your own if you have a phobia in *this* area. Doctors are likely to diagnose your problem as something other than a phobia.

In any case your first trips will be brief, because as soon as you *do* this strange feat, out of your mind will come the thought that it is not possible. It *is* possible, of course, because you are *doing* it. But the mind is subject to conditioning as well as logic, and conditioning can be anti-empirical.

This thought, which arises automatically out of the unconscious mind, serves as a suggestion or order *to* the unconscious mind, countermanding the original suggestion which got you 'out' in the first place. The result is that you snap back into the body so quickly that you may not be completely certain you ever got out in the first place.

My first experiences were like flash bulbs popping without warning in a completely darkened room. It was only *after* the projection was completed that I realized I had been successful in the first place. Later experiences lasted for a few seconds, and then for a few minutes. As Sax Rohmer says, 'the tyro cannot travel far.'[1] He should have written that in capital letters.

After you have reached a certain stage of development – after, say, you can project twelve feet (3.5 metres) and remain there for ten minutes, you are ready for the next step – astral meditation.

This is like ordinary meditation, the difference being that you are immediately outside the influence of your own physical aura when you do it. It is necessary to be able to get out first, and to stay out for a useful period of time to do this, but there are benefits to be derived, the nature of which I shall leave for you to discover.

Now it might be said that you will never find yourself able to project entirely at will. Psychic abilities are cantankerous, and as Israel Regardie pointed out in *The Tree of Life*, 'sometimes (the Astral Body) simply will not go.'[2] For what it is worth, this problem is shared even by the Masters.

In *The Occult World*, A. P. Sinnett relates an incident in which the
Master Morya tried to project himself, but was unsuccessful in doing so.
It was January, Sinnett was in Bombay, and Morya

> came to wish that I should have the satisfaction of seeing him in the
> Astral Body. [He] would have arranged for this, had the atmospherical
> and other conditions permitted it. But, unfortunately for me, these
> were not favourable. As M. wrote in one of several little notes I
> received him during that day and the following morning, even the
> Brothers, could not 'work miracles', and though to the ordinary
> spectator there may be but little difference between a miracle and
> some of the phenomena that the Brothers do sometimes accomplish,
> these latter are really results achieved by the manipulation of natural
> laws and forces, and are subject to obstacles which are sometimes
> practically insuperable.[3]

What is true for the Masters is true for the traveller on the astral
plane.

Just why this should be is a mystery – like much else about projection.
Sinnett believed that 'the production of phenomena' was 'immeasurably
easier' at the headquarters of the Theosophical Society than elsewhere
because of 'the constant presence of Madame Blavatsky and one or two
other persons of highly sympathetic magnetism, the purity of life of all
habitually resident there, and the constant influences poured in by the
Brothers themselves.' However, this would only explain why M. had
difficulty *manifesting* himself. We still have to explain why at times it is
impossible to 'get out'.

The ancients believed that it had to do with planetary or astrological
influences. In fact, it is this belief – that the astral body is affected by the
movement of the planets – that gives us the name *astral* body. The word
'astral' means 'having to do with the stars'. Paracelsus and other writers
have also used such words as 'sidereal' and 'celestial'. It is in fact through
this 'astral' or 'star' body that ancient astrologers assumed the planets
influenced human affairs.

Now there are seven astrological planets, but the one whose
influence is most undisputed is the moon. Anyone who has ever bathed
in the surf can see clearly the influence that the moon has on earthly
affairs, and for this and other reasons it is believed that the moon is the
chief among the 'planets' in the intensity of its astral influence.

In *The Llewellyn Practical Guide to Astral Projection*, Melita Denning and

Osborne Phillips say that the waxing phase of the moon is the best time to practise projection. One should avoid projecting during the waning phase in the opinion of these authors, and one should also avoid what they call the 'dead' period of the year – between December 21 and March 22.[4]

The AMORC Rosicrucians, who teach essentially the same thing about the moon and projection, have what seems to me to be a more scientific suggestion. They encourage their students to keep a diary of their experiences, not paying any attention to the phases of the moon particularly, but noting the dates on which their greatest successes occur. After numerous observations have been made and recorded, the diary can be checked against an almanac, to see if any lunar influence is discernible.

Now there is another way in which we can make use of these astrological connections, and that is through the so-called 'astrological' Sutras of Patanjali.

Those of you who have read my previous books on *Levitation* and *Invisibility* know that Patanjali was an early sage who wrote a book of terse verse concerning yoga, a book which has become known as the *Yoga Sutras*. This text is undoubtedly the definitive classic work on yoga, particularly the mental side of yoga, and the third book, which has to do with the *siddhis*, or occult powers, is probably the most complete manual of occult technique ever written. Patanjali maintains that by performing a yogic exercise called *Sanyama* on certain prescribed objects one may acquire any occult ability he might desire. And three of these exercises are directed at the heavenly bodies.

The whole subject of *Sanyama* is a complicated one, and one which I dealt with at length in my book on *Levitation*. I shall therefore not repeat myself here. Suffice it to say that *Sanyama* is prolonged concentration on a specific object – prolonged with the express purpose of producing yogically interesting alterations in the awareness of the concentrator. That these alterations are possible is an experimental fact, although some of them would seem strange indeed to anyone hearing of them for the first time. One of these *Sanyamas* has to do with projection into other planes of existence.

Patanjali says, in the twenty-sixth *Sutra* of Book Three, that 'as a result of *Sanyama* on the Sun, the yogi acquires knowledge of the Realms.'

Now that is all Patanjali says, but, as with the other *Sutras*, Vyasa goes much further.

He says that in the yogic system, there are seven realms, or *Lokas*. The lowest of these includes the six hells, which represent the 'excesses' of earth, air, fire, water, *akasa*, and darkness.[5] 'Here are born beings which are to suffer from the consequences of their stored up Karma', says Vyasa.[6] Above that are the seven 'nether worlds', then five other 'Realms' which correspond to the five stages of the development of matter, according to yoga. The earth is the first of these, corresponding to the *Maha-bhutas*, or gross elements. This is followed by the realm of generic characteristics, then the *tanmantras*, the Gunas, and finally the Self. In Rama Prasad's translation, Vyasa refers to the sun as an *entrance*, but in Wood's translation the word used is *door*, and with that we see how the *Solar Sanyama* is performed.[7]

MacGregor Mathers of the Hermetic Order of the Golden Dawn received credit for figuring this one out, and although he used 'Elemental' symbols, or *Tattwa* symbols instead of the sun, the procedure is the same.

One must not stare at the sun in the sky, obviously, because this can cause irreparable retinal damage to the eye. What you do is *visualize* the sun, just as you would visualize one of the GD *Tattwa* symbols, and as you visualize it, imagine that it is slowly growing in size, until it is the size of a doorway into another dimension. When you feel that you have reached this stage, mentally 'step through' the solar doorway and *close it behind you*. This last step will enhance the quality of the experience. Then, look around and see what you can see.

At first, your visions will be vague, but in time they will increase in intensity, until at last – so say the yogis – you will be able to 'see' all the realms I have just described. The GD manuscripts suggest that you should carefully note your path after entering through the doorways, and 'return' by the same path. In other words, after completing a 'trip' do not just open your eyes as you might if you were projecting onto *this* plane instead of another. This is particularly important if you are exploring some of the inferior regions, for reasons that will become clear as you experiment. On each occasion, make a note of the time and date, and above all, as Vyasa says, *'practise*, until all becomes clear.'[8]

Appendix A

The Adventures of Er, the Pamphylian, in the Other World from The Republic of Plato

Translated by Benjamin Jowett

Well, I said I will tell you a tale; not one of the tales which Odysseus tells
to the hero Alcinous, yet this, too, is a tale of a hero, Er, the son of
Armenius, a Pamphylian by birth. He was slain in battle, and ten days
afterward, when the bodies of the dead were taken up already in a state
of corruption, his body was found unaffected by decay, and carried away
home to be buried. And on the twelfth day, as he was lying on the
funeral pyre, he returned to life and told them what he had seen in the
other world. He said that when his soul left his body he went on a
journey with a great company, and that they came to a mysterious place
at which there were two openings in the earth. They were near together,
and over against them were two other openings in the heaven above. In
the intermediate space there were judges seated, who commanded the
just, after they had given judgement on them and had bound their
sentences in front of them, to ascend by the heavenly way on the right
hand. And in like manner the unjust were bidden by them to descend by
the lower way on the left hand. These also bore the symbols of their
deeds, but fastened on their backs. He drew near, and they told him that
he was to be the messenger who would carry the report of the Other
World to men, and they bade him hear and see all that was to be heard
and seen in that place. Then he beheld and saw on one side the souls
departing at either opening of heaven and earth when sentence had been
given on them. And at the two other openings other souls, some
ascending out of the earth dusty and worn with travel, some descending
out of heaven clean and bright. And arriving ever and anon they seemed
to have come from a long journey, and they went forth with gladness
into the meadow, where they encamped as at a festival. And those who
knew one another embraced and conversed, the souls which came to
earth curiously inquiring about the things above, and the souls which
came from heaven about the things beneath. And they told one another

of what had happened by the way, those from below weeping and sorrowing at the remembrance of the things which they had endured and seen in their journey beneath the earth (which journey lasted a thousand years), while those from above were describing heavenly delights and visions of inconceivable beauty. The story, Glaucon, would take too long to tell. But the sum was this: he said that for every wrong which they had done to any one they suffered tenfold, or once in a hundred years – such being reckoned to be the length of a man's life, and the penalty being thus paid ten times in a thousand years. If, for example, there were any who had been the cause of many deaths, or had betrayed or enslaved cities or armies, or been guilty of any other evil behaviour, for each and all of their offences they received punishment ten times over, and the rewards of beneficence and justice and holiness were in the same proportion. I need hardly repeat what he said concerning young children dying almost as soon as they were born. Of piety and impiety to gods and parents, and of murderers, there were retributions other and greater far which he described. He mentioned that he was present when one of the spirits asked another, 'Where is Aridaeus the Great?' Now this Aridaeus lived a thousand years before the time of Er. He had been the tyrant of some city of Pamphylia, and had murdered his aged father and his elder brother, and was said to have committed many other abominable crimes. The answer of the other spirit was: 'He comes not hither and will never come.' And this, said he, 'was one of the dreadful sights which we ourselves witnessed. We were at the mouth of the cavern, and having completed all our experiences, were about to reascend, when of a sudden Aridaeus appeared and several others, most of whom were tyrants. And there were also besides the tyrants more individuals who had been great criminals. They were just, as they fancied, about to return into the upper world, but the mouth, instead of admitting them, gave a roar, whenever any of these incurable sinners, or someone who had not been sufficiently punished, tried to ascend. And then wild men of fiery aspect, who were standing by and heard the sound, seized [them] and carried them off. And Aridaeus and others they bound foot and hand, and threw them down and flayed them with scourges, and dragged them along the road at the side, carding them on thorns like wool, and declaring to the passers-by what were their crimes, and that they were being taken away to be cast into hell.' And of all the many terrors which they had endured, he said that there was none like the terror which each of them felt at that moment, lest they should hear the voice. And when there was silence, one by one they ascended with exceeding joy. These, said Er, were the penalties and retributions, and there were blessings as great.

Now when the spirits which were in the meadow had tarried seven days, on the eighth they were obliged to proceed on their journey, and, on the fourth day after, he said that they came to a place where they could see from above a line of light, straight as a column, extending right through the whole heaven and through the earth, in colour resembling the rainbow, only brighter and purer. Another day's journey brought them to the place, and there, in the midst of the light, they saw the ends of the chains of heaven let down from above. For this light is the belt of heaven, and holds together the circle of the universe, like the undergirders of a trireme. From this end is extended the spindle of Necessity, on which all the revolutions turn.

When Er and the [other] spirits arrived, their duty was to go at once to Lachesis [one of the three Fates, who, according to Plato, sings of the past]. But first of all there came a prophet who arranged them in order. Then he took from the knees of Lachesis lives and samples of lives, and having mounted a high pulpit, spoke as follows, 'Hear the words of Lachesis, the daughter of Necessity. Mortal souls, behold a new cycle of life and mortality. Your genius will not be allotted to you, but you will choose your genius, and let him who draws the first lot have the first choice, and the life which he chooses shall be his destiny. Virtue is free, and as a man honours or dishonours her he will have more or less of her. The responsibility is with the chooser – God is justified.' When the Interpreter had thus spoken he scattered lots indifferently among them all, and each of them took up the lot which fell near him, all but Er himself (he was not allowed). Each as he took his lot perceived the number which he had obtained. Then the Interpreter placed on the ground before them the samples of lives, and there were many more lives than [there were] souls present, and they were all sorts. There were lives of every animal and of man in every condition. And there were tyrannies among them, some lasting out the tyrant's life, others which broke in the middle and came to an end in poverty and exile and beggary. And there were lives of famous men, some of whom were famous for their form and beauty as well as for their strength and success in games, or, again, for their birth and the qualities of their ancestors, and some who were the reverse of famous for the opposite qualities. And of women likewise. There was not, however, any definite character in them, because the soul, when choosing a new life, must of necessity become different. But there was every other quality, and they all mingled with one another, and also with elements of wealth and poverty, and disease and health. And there were mean states also. And according to the messenger from the other world, this is what the prophet said at the time. 'Even for the last comer, if he chooses wisely and will live diligently, there is appointed a happy and not an undesirable existence. Let not him who chooses first be careless, and let not the last despair.' When he had spoken, he who had the first choice came forward, and in a moment chose the greatest tyranny. His mind having been darkened by folly and sensuality, he had not thought the whole matter out before he chose, and did not at first sight perceive that he was fated, among other evils, to devour his own children. But when he had time to reflect, and saw what was in the lot, he began to beat his breast and lament over his choice, forgetting the proclamation of the prophet. For, instead of throwing the blame of his misfortune on himself, he accused chance and the gods and everything rather than himself. Now he was one of those who came from heaven, and in a former life had dwelt in a well-ordered State. But his virtue was a matter of habit only, and he had no philosophy. Of others who were similarly overtaken, the greater number came from heaven and therefore had never been schooled by trial, whereas the pilgrims who came from earth, having themselves suffered and seen others suffer, were not in a hurry to choose. And owning to this inexperience of theirs, and also because the lot was a chance, many of the souls exchanged a good destiny for an evil one, or an evil destiny for a good one. For if a man had always on his arrival in this world dedicated himself from the first to sound philosophy, and had been moderately fortunate in the number of the lot, he might, as the messenger reported, be happy here, and also his journey to another life would be smooth and heavenly, instead of being rough and underground. The spectacle was most curious, said he, for the choice of the souls was in most cases based on their experience of a previous life. About the middle came the lot of Atlanta. She, seeing the great fame of an athlete, was unable to resist the temptation. And after her followed the soul of Epeus the son of Panopeus passing into the nature of a woman cunning in the arts. There came also the soul of Odysseus, having yet to make a choice, and his lot happened to be the last of them all. The recollection of former toils had disenchanted him of ambition, and he went about for a considerable time in search of the life of a private man who had no cares. He had some difficulty in finding this, which was lying about and had been neglected by everybody else. And when he saw it, he said that he would have done the same had his lot been first instead of last, and that he was delighted to have it. All the souls had now chosen their lives, and they went in order of their choice to Lachesis, who sent with them the genius which they had severally chosen, to be the guardian of their lives and the fulfiller of the choice. This genius led the soul first to Clotho, and drew them within the revolution of the spindle impelled by her hand, thus ratifying the destiny of each, and then, when they were fastened to this, to Atropos, who spun the threads and made them irreversible, whence without turning they passed beneath the Throne of Necessity. And when they had all passed, they marched on in a scorching heat to the plain of Forgetfulness, which was a barren waste, destitute of trees and verdure, and then towards evening they camped by the river of Unmindfulness, whose waters no vessel may hold. Of this they were all obliged to drink a certain quantity, and those who were not saved by wisdom drank more than was necessary. And as each one drank he forgot all things.

After they had gone to rest, about the middle of the light, there was a thunderstorm and an earthquake, and they were driven upwards in all manner of ways to their birth, like stars shooting through the sky. Er himself was hindered from drinking the water. But in what manner or by what means he returned, he could not say. Only, in the morning, awakening suddenly, he found himself lying on a funeral pyre.

Appendix B

The Experience of Timarchus in the Other World from Plutarch

The following story is found in Plutarch's essay entitled 'A Discourse Concerning Socrates' Daemon'. I have reserved it for an Appendix because it seems to me to be an inferior vision, yet interesting enough not to be left out altogether. The Greeks used the word 'daemon' differently than we do today. To them it did not mean 'evil spirit', but rather the higher part of ourselves – that part of the self which inspires us, which manifests ESP and intuition, and which passes forth from the body during astral projection, while the soul remains behind. Socrates especially is said to have consulted his 'daemon' constantly, especially in matters of philosophy, and to have been well satisfied with the results. The 'daemon', if you will, is the 'still, small voice' from within.

The Oracle of Trophonius, which is also mentioned in this vision, was a cave at Lebadea in Boeotia. According to Bullfinch, it was discovered during a great drought. He says

> The Boetians were directed by the god at Delphi to seek aid of Trophonius at Lebadea. They came thither, but could find no oracle. One of them, however, happening to see a swarm of bees, followed them to a chasm in the earth, which proved to be the place sought. Peculiar ceremonies were to be performed by the person who came to consult the oracle. After these preliminaries, he descended into the cave by a narrow passage. This place could be entered only in the night. The person retreated from the cave by the same narrow passage, but walking backwards. He appeared melancholy and dejected. And hence the proverb which was applied to a person low-spirited and gloomy. 'He has been consulting the oracle of Trophonius'.

Now Plutarch says that Timarchus, who had the vision, emerged from Trophonius' cave with a *cheerful* countenance, possibly because of the revelations he experienced therein. Timarchus was one of the pupils of Socrates, a man who died very young, and who asked Socrates if he might be buried next to Socrates' son Lampocles, his dear friend during life. Plutarch puts the account of the vision into the mouth of Simmias, who tells it to Theocritus in the following words:

Timarchus, being eager to know what Socrates' daemon was, [and] acquainting none but Cebes and me with his design, went down ino Trophonius' cave, and performed all the ceremonies that were requisite to gain an oracle. There he stayed two nights and one day, so that his friends despaired of his return, and lamented him as lost. But the next morning he came out with a very cheerful countenance, and having adored the god, and freed himself from the thronging, inquisitive crowd, he told us many wonderful things that he had seen and heard. For this was his relation. As soon as he entered, a thick darkness surrounded him. He felt that he had struck his head, and that through the parted sutures of his skull his soul flew out, which, now being loose and mixed with a purer and lighter air, was most jocund and well pleased. It seemed to begin to breathe, as if formerly it had been choking, and it grew in size, like a sail swollen by the wind. Then he heard a small noise whirling about his head, very sweet and ravishing. Looking up he saw no earth, but instead saw innumerable islands, unequal in size, but completely surrounding him, shining with a gentle fire, and changing colours with the variation in the light. The whirling of the islands, it is likely, agitated the ether, and made the sound, for the ravishing softness of it was very agreeable to their even motions. Between these islands there was a large sea or lake, which shone very gloriously, being adorned with a gay variety of colours mixed with blue. Some few of the islands swam in the sea, and were carried to the other side of the current. Others, and these were the most, were carried up and down, tossed, whirled, and almost overwhelmed. The sea in some places seemed very deep, especially toward the south, and in others very shallow. It ebbed and flowed, but the tides were neither high nor strong. In some parts its colour was pure and sea-green. In others it looked troubled and muddy as a pool. The current brings those islands that were carried over to the other side back again, but not to the same point, so that their motions are not exactly circular but winding. About the middle of these islands, the ambient sea seemed to bend into a hollow, a little less, as it appeared to him, than eight parts of the whole. Into this sea were two entrances, by which it received two opposite fiery rivers, running in with so strong a current that it spread a fiery white over a great part of the blue sea. The sight pleased him very much, but when he looked downward, there appeared a vast chasm. It was round, as if he had looked into a divided sphere, very deep and frightful, full of thick darkness, which was every now and then troubled and disturbed. Thence a thousand howlings and bellowings of beasts, cries of children, moans of men and women, and all sorts of terrible noises reached his ears, but faintly, as being far off and rising through the vast hollow, and this terrified him exceedingly. A little while after, an invisible Being spoke thus to him:

'Timarchus, what do you wish to understand?' And he replied: 'Everything, for what is there here that is not wonderful and surprising?'

'We have little to do with those things above', said the Being, 'for they belong to other gods, but as for Proserpina's quarter – which is one of the four quarters, as the River Styx divides them – that we govern, and you may visit if you wish.'

'But what is Styx?'

'The way to hell, which reaches to the contrary quarter, and with its head divides the light. For, as you see, it rises from hell below, and as it rolls on touches also the light, and is the extreme limit of the Universe. There are four divisions of all things. The first is of life, the second of motion, the third of generation, and the fourth of corruption. The first is coupled to the second by a unit, invisible in substance. The second [is coupled] to the third by understanding, in the Sun, and the third to the fourth by Nature, in the Moon. Over each of these ties a Fate presides. Over the first, Atropos, over the second, Clotho, and over the third, Lachesis, who is in the Moon, and about whom is the third whirl of generation. All the other islands have gods in them; but the Moon, belonging to earthly daemons, is raised but a little above the Styx. Styx seizes upon her once in an hundred and seventy-seven second revolutions, and when it approaches the souls are startled, and cry out for fear; for hell swallows up a great many, and the Moon receives some swimming up from below which have run through their whole course of generation, unless they are wicked and impure. For against such she throws flashes of lightning, makes horrible noises, and frightens them away, so that, missing their desired happiness and bewailing their condition, they are carried down again to undergo another generation.'

'But', said Timarchus, 'I see nothing but stars leaping about the hollow, some carried into it, and some darting out of it again.'

'These', said the Voice, 'are daemons; for thus it is. Every soul hath some portion of reason. A man cannot be a man without it. But as much of each soul as is mixed with flesh and appetite is changed, and through pain or pleasure becomes irrational. Every soul doth not mix herself after one sort; for some plunge into the body, and so in this life their whole frame is corrupted by appetite and passion. Others are mixed as to some part, but the purer part still remains without the body. It is not drawn down into it, but swims above, and touches the extremest part of man's head. It is like a *cord* to hold up and direct the subsiding part of the soul, as long as it proves obedient and is not overcome by the appetites of the flesh. That part that is plunged into the body is called the soul, but the uncorrupted part is called the mind, and the vulgar think it is within them, as likewise they imagine the reflected image to be within the glass. But the more intelligent, who know it to be without, call it a *daemon*. Therefore, those stars which you see extinguished, imagine to be souls whose whole substances are plunged into bodies. And those that recover their light and rise from below, that shake off the ambient darkness, as if it were clay and dirt, know to be such as retire from their bodies after death. And those that are carried up on high are the daemons of wise men and philosophers. But pray pry narrowly and endeavour to discover the tie by which everyone is united to a soul.'

Upon this, Timarchus looked as steadfastly as he could, and saw some of the stars very much agitated, and some less, as corks upon a net, and some whirled round like a spindle, having a very irregular and uneven motion, not being able to run in a straight line. And to this the Voice said: 'Those that have a straight and regular motion belong to souls which are very manageable, by reason of their genteel breeding and philosophical education, and which upon earth do not plunge themselves into the foul clay and become irrational. But those that move irregularly, sometimes upwards, sometimes downwards, as striving to break loose from a vexing chain, are yoked to and strive with very intractable conditions, which ignorance and want of learning make headstrong and ungovernable. Sometimes they get the better of the passions, and draw them to the right side. Sometimes they are drawn away by them, and sink into sin and folly, and then again endeavour to get out. For the tie is, as it were a bridle on the

irrational part of the soul, and when it is pulled back, draws in
repentance for past sins, and shame for loose and unlawful pleasures,
which is a pain and stroke inflicted upon the soul by a governing and
prevailing power. By this means it becomes gentle and manageable,
and like a tamed beast, without blows or torment, it understands the
minutest direction of the daemon. Such indeed are but very slowly
and very hardly brought to a right temper, but of that sort which from
the very beginning are governable and obedient to the direction of
the daemon, are those prophetic souls, those intimates of the gods.
Such was the soul of Hermodorus the Clazomenian, of which it is
reported that for several days and nights it would leave his body,
travel over many countries, and return after it had viewed things and
discoursed with persons at a great distance, till at last, by the
treachery of his wife, his body was delivered to his enemies, and they
burned his house while he was 'out'. It is certain that this is mere
fable. For the soul never went out of the body, but loosened the tie
that held the daemon, and permitted it to wander, so that the daemon,
seeing and hearing, brought the news back to the soul. Yet those that
burned his body are even to this time severely tormented in the
deepest pit of hell. But this, youth, you shall more clearly perceive
three months hence; now depart.'

The voice continuing no longer, Timarchus [as he said] turned
around to discover who it was who had spoken, but a violent pain
seized his head, as if his skull had been pressed together, so that he lost
all sense and understanding. But in a little while recovering, he found
himself in the entrance of the cave, where he at first lay down.

Appendix C
The Experiences of Thespesius of Soli in the Other World as told by Plutarch

This story is the last of our little trilogy of ancient Greek near death experiences. It differs from more modern accounts by the extreme moralism of the storyteller, and this makes me suspicious that the story may have been improved upon before being set down in writing. Yet numerous interesting points are made in this story, which make it unlikely to be completely made up, among them the very first reference to the so-called 'silver cord' to be found anywhere in world literature. It was left to us by Plutarch, and is found in Clough's edition of Plutarch's collected works. I give it here for what it is worth.

There was one Thespesius of Soli, the friend and familiar acquaintance of that Protogenes who for some time conversed among us. This gentleman in his youth led a debauched and intemperate life, in a short time spent his patrimony, and then for some years became very wicked, but afterwards repented of his former follies and extravagances, and pursuing the recovery of his lost estate by all manner of tricks and shifts, did as is usual with dissolute and lascivious youths, who, when they have wives of their own, never mind them at all, but when they have dismissed them, and find them married to others that watch them with a more vigilant affection, endeavour to corrupt and vitiate them by all the unjust and wicked provocations imaginable. In this humour, abstaining from nothing that was lewd and illegal, so it tended to his gain and profit, he got no great manner of wealth, but procured to himself a world of infamy by his unjust and knavish dealing with all sorts of people. Yet nothing made him more the talk of the country, than the answer which was brought him back from the oracle of Amphilocus. For thither it seems he sent to inquire of the god whether he should live any better during the remainder of his life, to which the oracle answered, that he would live better after he had died. And indeed, not long after the thing came true. For he happened to fall from a certain precipice upon his neck, and though he received no wound nor broke any limb, yet the force of the fall knocked the wind out of him. Three days after, being carried forth to be buried, just as he was about to be let into the grave, suddenly he came to himself, and recovered his strength, and so altered the course of his life, that it was almost incredible to those who knew him. For by the report of the Cilicians, there never was in that age a more just person in common dealings between man and man, or more devout and religious as to divine worship, or more an enemy to the wicked, or more constant and faithful to his friends.

For that reason, those who knew him well wanted to hear from him the cause of such a great alteration, not believing that such a thing could come about by mere chance, though it seems that it did just that, as he related to Protogenes and others of his closest friends.

For when his sense left his body, he felt as he would if he had been a pilot flung from the helm of his ship and into the sea by the force of a storm. Afterwards, rising up again above water by degrees, so soon as he thought he had fully recovered his breath, he looked about him every way, as if one eye of his soul had been opened. But he beheld none of the things which he formerly had been wont to see. Instead, he saw stars of vast magnitude, at immense distances from one another, and sending forth a light most wonderful for the brightness of its colour, which shot itself out in length with incredible force, on which the soul, riding as it were in a chariot, was most swiftly, yet as gently and smoothly, dandled from one place to another. But omitting the greatest part of the sights that he beheld, he saw, as he said, the souls of such as were newly dead, as they mounted from below, resembling little fiery bubbles, to which the air gave way. These bubbles afterwards broke insensibly and by degrees, the soul coming forth from them in the shapes of men and women, light and nimble, as being discharged of all earthly substance. However, they differed in their motion. For some of them leaped forth with a wonderful swiftness, and mounted up in a direct line. Others, like so many spindles of spinning-wheels turned round and round, sometimes whirling upwards, sometimes darting downwards, with a confused and mixed agitation, that could hardly be stopped in a very long time.'

'He did not know most of these souls, but, perceiving two or three of his acquaintance, he endeavoured to approach and talk to them.

But they neither heard him speak, nor, for that matter, did they seem to be in their right mind, fluttering and out of their senses, disdaining either to be seen or felt. They frisked up and down at first, alone and apart by themselves, till meeting at length with others in the same condition, they clung together. But still their motions were with the same giddiness and uncertainty as before, without steerage or purpose. And they made sounds like the cries of soldiers in combat, intermixed with doleful yells of fear and lamentation. Others towered aloft in the upper region of the air, and these looked gay and pleasant, and frequently accosted each other with kindness and respect. They shunned the troubled souls, and seemed to show discontent by crowding together, and joy and pleasure by expanding and separating from each other. One of these, said he, being the soul of a certain kinsman, whom he did not know well, the person having died when very young, drew near him, and saluted him by the name of Thespesius. At this he was amazed, and said that his name was not Thespesius but Aridaeus, whereupon the spirit replied, "it was true that you were once called that, but from now on you shall be called Thespesius, which is to say, 'divine'. For you are not numbered among the dead yet, but by a certain Destiny and permission of the gods you are come here with only your Mind, having left the rest of your soul, like an anchor, in your body. And that you may be assured of this, observe that the souls of the dead do not cast a shadow or open and shut their eyelids." Thespesius, having heard this, was so much the more encouraged to make use of his own reason. And looking around to perceive the truth of what he had been told, he saw that a kind of obscure and shadowlike line followed him, whereas the other souls shone like a round body of perfect light, and were transparent within. And yet there was a very great difference between even those. For some yielded a smooth, even, and continuous lustre, all of one colour, like the full moon in her brightest splendour, and others were marked with long scales or slender streaks. Still others were covered with black speckles like the skins of vipers, and there were yet others who were marked by faint scratches.'

'At this Thespesius' kinsman told him several things, how that Adrastea, daughter of Jupiter and of Necessity, sat in the highest place of all, to punish every sort of crime. And that in the whole number of the wicked and ungodly, there was not one – great or little, high or low, rich or poor – who could escape by force or cunning the severe lashes of her rigour. But as there are three sorts of punishments, so there are three Furies, or female ministers of Justice; and to each of these belongs a particular office and degree of punishment. The first of these was called Speedy Punishment [Poine], who takes charge of those who are to receive punishment while still in the body, and who she manages in a gentle manner, ignoring many offences which need expiation. If a greater labour is required, they are delivered to Justice [Dike], and if Dike has given them up as incorrigible, then the third and most severe of all Adrastea's ministers, Erinnys, takes them in hand. And after she has chased them from one place to another, flying, yet not knowing where to go for shelter or relief, plagued and tormented with a thousand miseries, she plunges them headlong into an invisible abyss, the hideousness of which no tongue can express.'

'Now of all these three sorts, that which is inflicted by punishment in this life resembles the practice among the barbarians. For as the Persians take off the garments and turbans of those they would punish, and tear and whip [the garments] before the offender's faces, while the criminals beg for mercy with tears and lamentations, so corporal punishments, mulcts, and fines, have no severity, and do not take hold of the vice itself, but are inflicted mostly with regard to appearances and the senses. But if anyone comes hither who has escaped punishment while he lived upon the earth, and before he was well purged from his crimes, Justice takes him to task, naked, with his soul in full view, and with nothing to conceal his criminality, but on all sides and to all men's eyes exposed, she shows him first to his honest parents, if he had any, that they may see how degenerate he was, and how unworthy of his progenitors. But if his parents were also wicked, then are their sufferings rendered yet more terrible by the mutual sight of each other's miseries, and this continues for a long time, until every crime has been effaced with torments which as much surpass the miseries of the flesh, as these surpass a mere idle dream. But the weals and stripes that remain after punishment appear more obvious in some, less evident in others.'

'See there, he said, the colours of different souls. The black and sordid hue is the colour of avarice and fraud. The bloody and flame-like colour betokens cruelty and lust for revenge. Where you see the bluish colour, it is a sign that the soul will hardly be cleansed from the impurities of lascivious pleasure and voluptuousness. Finally, the dark, violet, and venemous colour, which resembles the ink spewed up by a cuttle fish, comes from envy. For as during life the wickedness of the soul, being governed by the passions and in turn governing the body, occasions this variety of colours; so here it is the end of expiation and punishment, when these are cleansed away, and the soul recovers her native lustre and becomes clear and spotless. But so long as these remain, there will be some certain returns of the passions, accompanied with little pantings and beatings, as it were of the pulse, in some remiss and languid, and quickly extinguished, and in others more quick and vehement. Some of these souls, being born again and again chastised, recover a due habit and disposition, while others, by the force of ignorance and the enticing show of pleasure, are carried into the bodies of brute beasts. For while some, through the feebleness of their reasoning ability, are compelled by their active principle to seek a new incarnation, others, lacking temperance, wish to gratify their desires. Here [on the astral plane] there is nothing but an imperfect shadow and dream of pleasure which cannot be realized.'

'Having said this, the spirit carried Thespesius to a certain place, where it appeared to him there were wide open spaces, yet so gently, that he seemed to be borne upon rays of light, as if upon wings. At last he came to a gaping chasm which appeared to be bottomless, and there found himself deserted by the extraordinary force that brought him there. He saw other souls there in the same condition as myself. They hovered in flocks like birds, flying around and around the mouth of the chasm, but not daring to enter. Within, the chasm resembled the groves of Bacchus, fringed about with the pleasing verdure of various herbs and plants, and yielding a delightful prospect of all sorts of flowers, interrupting the greenness with a wonderful variety of colours, and at the same time offering a gentle breeze, which graced the air with perfumes as delightful to the souls as the fragrance of wines is to us on earth. The souls which partook of these fragrances were almost all dissolved in raptures of mirth and caresses. There was nothing to be heard for some distance but laughter, and all the sounds of merriment which are common among those who pass their time in sport.'

'The spirit said that Bacchus ascended by this route to heaven, and afterwards returning fetched Semele the same way. It was called the Place of Oblivion [Lethe]. He would therefore not suffer Thespesius to tarry there, and carried him away against his will, instructing him by this experience how easily the mind is carried away by pleasure, and that the irrational part, having thus been awakened, revives the memory of the body. From this proceeds desire and an appetite for reincarnation. It occurs when the soul is weighed down with too much moisture.'

'After he had been carried the same distance in the other direction, Thespesius thought he saw an enormous goblet, into which several rivers emptied. Among them was one which was whiter than snow. Another resembled a rainbow. The tinctures of the rest were varied. As he drew nearer, the air became more rarefied and the colours disappeared, so that the goblet was perfectly white, and he saw three daemons sitting together in a triangular formation, mixing the rivers together in certain measures. Thus far, said Thespesius' guide, did Orpheus come when he sought for the soul of his wife. When he returned to earth, he remembered what he had seen only imperfectly, and popularized a false conception. Orpheus said that the Delphic oracle was common to Night and Apollo, whereas Apollo never had anything to do with Night. But, said he spirit, the oracle is common to Night and the Moon, which is not within the earth's boundaries, and has no fixed or certain seat, but wanders among men in dreams and visions. For it is for this reason that dreams are confused, compounded as they are of truth and falsehood intermixed. But concerning the oracle of Apollo, said the spirit, you neither see it, nor can behold it. For the earthbound part of the soul cannot let itself loose, and therefore cannot ascend to sublimity [Devachan], but tends earthward, being fastened to the body.'

'With that, leading Thespesius nearer, the spirit endeavoured to show him the light of the Tripod, which, as he said, fell upon Parnassus after shooting through the bosom of Themis. Thespesius wanted to see this, but could not, since he was dazzled by the extraordinary brilliance of the light. Passing by, he heard the shrill voice of a woman speaking in verse, and, as he thought, foretelling the time of his own death, among other things. This, the spirit told him, was the voice of a Sybil, who was whirled about in orbit across the face of the Moon, and who continually sang of future events. He wanted to hear more but he was tossed in the opposite direction by the motion of the Moon, as by the force of rolling waves, so that he could hear very little, and that only in bits and pieces. Among other things, he heard prophecies concerning Mount Vesuvius, and the destruction of Dicaearchia by fire, together with a fragment of verse concerning an emperor of his time,

'Who, though so just that no man could accuse,

However, his empire should by sickness lose.'

'After this, they passed on to see the torments of the dammed, and they did indeed see some dismal sights. Thespesius unexpectedly found himself among his friends and relatives, who were groaning and who called him by name. At length he saw his father ascending from a certain abyss, covered with stripes, gashes, and scars. He was not permitted to keep silence, but was compelled to make confession by his tormentors, and, stretching out his hands, admitted that he had poisoned some of his guests for the sake of their gold. He had gone undetected in life, but was convicted in death, and had already undergone some of his punishments, and was being summoned to a place where he would undergo even more. Thespesius was so frightened by this that he did not dare intercede on his father's behalf. He wanted very much to leave, and looked around for his guide, but he was nowhere to be seen.'

'He was pushed forward by deformed and grim-faced goblins, and found that the shadows of those who had been notorious criminals in this life and had been punished in life, were not punished so grievously as the others, nor even in the same manner, for their tendency toward vice comes from an imperfection in the irrational part of their soul. As for those who concealed their vice with an outward show of virtue, their tormentors turned them inside out, causing them great pain, like the sea scolopenders, which, having swallowed a hook, throw out their bowels and lick it out again. Others they flayed and terrified, to bring their secret hypocrisies and latent impieties, which possessed and corrupted the principal part of their souls, into the open. Still others he saw, who were intertwined in twos and threes, and who devoured each other, either because of ancient grudges, or else in revenge for injuries suffered while on earth.'

'Moreover, he said that there were certain lakes, equidistant one from the other, one of boiling cold, another of frozen lead, and still another of scaly and rugged iron. By the sides of these stood certain daemons with instruments, who lowered and raised the souls of avaricious and greedy men like smiths in a forge. For the flame of the golden furnace having rendered these souls of a fiery and transparent colour, they plunged them into that of lead, where, after they were congealed and hardened into a substance like hail, they were thrown into the lake of iron, where they became black and deformed, and being broken and crumbled by the roughness of the iron, changed their form. In all these transformations they endured the most dreadful torments. But they who suffered the most were those who believed that the divine vengeance had no more in store for them, and were seized and dragged to further execution. And these were those for whom their posterity suffered. For when any of the souls of those children meet those of their parents or ancestors, they fly into a rage, and accuse them, and show them the marks of what they have endured. The parents try to hide themselves, but the others follow them, and lay such bitter taunts upon them, that their tormentors lay hold of them and take them to new torments, howling and yelling at the very thought of what they have endured already. He said that as they murmured their complaints, some of these souls of posterity swarmed together like bees or bats.'

'The last things he saw were the souls of those who were destined for reincarnation. They were bowed, bent, and transformed into all sorts of creatures with tools and anvils which certain workmen, appointed for the purpose, used without mercy, bruising the limbs of some, breaking those of others, disjointing others, and pounding still others to powder, to render them fit for other lives. Among them he saw the soul of Nero being grievously tortured in many ways, but especially by being transfixed with nails. This soul the workmen took in hand, but when they had forged it into the form of one of Pindar's vipers, which eats its way to life through the bowels of the female, suddenly a conspicuous light shone forth, and a voice was heard out of the light, which ordered the soul transfigured again into some other, more gentle, creature, and so they made it to resemble one of the creatures that sing and croak at the sides of ponds and marshes. For indeed he had been punished in some measure for his crimes, and besides, the gods owed him some compassion. He restored the Greeks to their liberty, and the Greeks were of all his subjects the most beloved of the gods.'

'As he was about to return [to his body], a woman, admirable for her form and stature, took him by the arm, saying, "Come hither, that thou mayest the better be able to retain the remembrance of what thou hast seen." With that, she was about to strike him with a small fiery wand, similar to the kind painters use, but another woman prevented her. And then he thought himself whirled away by a strong and violent wind and forced as it were through a pipe. And so, lighting again into his own body, he awoke and found himself on the brink of his own grave.'

References

CHAPTER 1:

1. John Keel, *Jadoo, the Black Magic of the Orient*. New York: Messner, 1957, p.14.
2. Madame Blavatsky, *Isis Unveiled*. Los Angeles, California: The Theosophy Company, 1968, vol.1, p.477.
3. *Ibid.*
4. *Ibid*, p.478.
5. *Ibid.*
6. Eliphas Levi, *Histoire de la Magie*. Paris, 1860.
7. Keel, p.16.
8. Dr Paul Brunton, *A Search In Secret Egypt*. New York: Samuel Weiser, 1980.
9. D. H. Rawcliffe, *Occult and Supernatural Phenomena*. New York: Dover, undated, p.283.
10. *Ibid*, p.277.
11. Keel, p.169.
12. Rawcliffe, pp.284-6.
13. Keel, p.172.
14. Edgar Allen Poe, *The Premature Burial* in *The Prose Tales of Edgar Allen Poe*. New York: J. Widdleton, 1878.
15. *Ibid.*
16. Alfred Gordon Bennett, *Focus On the Unknown*. London: Rider, 1953, p.249.
17. Dr James Douglas Ward, 'Suspended Animation', in *The Rosicrucian Digest*, August 1931, pp.551-561.
18. F. W. H. Myers, *Human Personality and Its Survival of Bodily Death*. London: Longmans, Green & Co., 1904, pp.315-321.

CHAPTER 2:

1. Cornelius Agrippa, *The Philosophy of Natural Magic*. London, 1650, pp.183-187.

2. Quoted by Blavatsky, *Isis Unveiled*, vol.1, p.485.
3. *Ibid*, note 1.
4. William James, *The Varieties of Religious Experience*. New York: New American Library, 1958, p.301.
5. Pliny, *Natural History*, Book vii, chapter ii.
6. Vittorio D. Macchioro, *From Orpheus to Paul*. London: Constable & Co., Ltd., 1930, p.13.
7. James, p.299n.
8. James, p.300n.
9. Thomas de Quincey, *The Confessions of an English Opium Eater*. London: J. M. Dent & Sons, 1967, pp.233-248.
10. Augustine, *The City of God*, translated by Thomas Merton and George Glenluce. New York: Random House, 1950, p.625.
11. Jung-Stilling, *Theory of Pneumatology*. London, 1834, pp.74 et seq.
12. Julius Sachse, *The German Pietists of Provincial Pennsylvania*. New York: AMS Press, 1970, pp.393-395.

CHAPTER 3:

1. Barruel, *Memoires Illustrating the History of Jacobinism*. London, 1798, vol.iv, pp.120-1.
2. *Ibid*.
3. F. W. H. Myers, *Human Personality and Its Survival of Bodily Death*. London: Longmans, Green & Co., 1904, p.219.
4. Immanuel Kant, 'Brief an Fraeulein Charlotte von Knobloch', appended to *Traeume der Geisterseher*, Leipzig, 1766.
5. Quoted by Signe Toksvig, *Emmanuel Swedenborg, Scientist and Mystic*. London: Faber and Faber, Ltd;, 1919, 1948, p.187.
6. Samuel Warren, *A Compendium of the Writings of Emmanuel Swedenborg*. New York: Swedenborg Foundation, Inc., 1974, pp.625-6.
7. *Ibid*.
8. Barruel, p.123.
9. *Ibid*. p.124.
10. *Ibid*.
11. Myers, p.219.
12. Theophilus Parsons, *Essays*. Boston: Otis Clapp, 1845, 1865, p.225.

CHAPTER 4:

1. Francesca Mario Guazzo, *Compendium Maleficarum*, translated by E. A. Ashwin. London: John Rodker, 1929, p.33.
2. H. C. Lea, *Materials Toward A History of Witchcraft*. New York and London: Thomas Yoseloff, 1957, p.151.
3. Guazzo, p.32.

4. Sprenger, *Malleus Maleficarum*, quoted by Reginald Scot, *Discoverie of Witchcraft*, London, 1651.
5. Lafcadio Hearn, 'Gaki', in *Katto, Japanese Curios, With Sundry Cobwebs*. New York: Macmillan, 1903.
6. Christopher Heywood, *The Life of Merlin, Surnamed Ambrosius*. London: Lackington, Allen & Co., 1813, pp.52-3.
7. *Ibid*, p.40.
8. Plutarch, *Life of Alexander*, translated by John Dryden, in *Plutarch's Lives*, vol.iv. New York: The Nottingham Society, undated.
9. T. W. Doane, *Bible Myths and Their Parallels in Other Religions*. New York: J. W. Bouton, 1882.
10. Dion Fortune, *Esoteric Philosophy of Love and Marriage*. Denington Estate, Wellingborough: The Aquarian Press, 1981, p.52.
11. *Ibid*, p.85.
12. Dion Fortune, *Psychic Self Defence*. Denington Estate, Wellingborough: The Aquarian Press, 1979, p.79.
13. Oliver Bland, *Adventures of a Modern Occultist*. New York: Dodd, Mead, and Co., 1920, p.92.
14. *Ibid*, p.81.
15. *Ibid*, p.82.
16. Barruel, *Memoires Illustrating the History of Jacobinism*. London, 1798, vol.iv, pp.122-3.
17. Madame Blavatsky, *Raja-Yoga, or Occultism*. Bombay: The Theosophy Company, 1931, pp.80-1.
18. *Ibid*, p.81.
19. *Ibid*, p.80.
20. *Ibid*, p.85.
21. *Ibid*.
22. Jules Bois, *Le Satanisme et la magie*. Paris: Ernest Flammarion, editeur, 1897, pp.235-6.
23. Reginald Scot, op. cit.
24. *Ibid*.
25. Daniel Defoe, *History of the Devil*. London: T. Kelley, 1819, pp.383-4.
26. Montague Summers, *The History of Witchcraft and Demonology*. New York: University Books, 1956, p.96.
27. George Lyman Kittredge, *Witchcraft in Old and New England*. New York: Russell and Russell, 1958, p.118.
28. W. B. Yeats, *Autobiographies*, New York: Macmillan, 1953, p.209.
29. Dion Fortune, 'Ceremonial Magic Unveiled', in *The Occult Review*, quoted by Israel Regardie in *My Rosicrucian Adventure*. Saint Paul, Minnesota: Llewellyn Publications, 1971, p.30.
30. *Ibid*, pp.30-1.
31. Ithell Colquhoun, *The Sword of Wisdom*. New York: G. P. Putnam's Sons, 1975, p.294.

32. Christina Mary Stoddart ('Inquire Within'), *Light Bearers of Darkness*. Hawthorne, California: The Christian Book Club of America, 1969, p.127.

33. Marion Meade, *Madame Blavatsky, the Woman Behind the Myth*. New York: G. P. Putnam's Sons, 1980, p.7.

34. Yeats, *Autobiographies*, p.109.

35. Meade, p.365.

36. Yeats, p.109.

37. Meade, p.422.

38. *Letters From the Masters of the Wisdom*, quoted by Meade, op. cit.

39. Kittredge, p.118.

40. *Proceedings of the Society for Psychic Research*, vol.12.

41. Melita Denning and Osborne Phillips, *The Llewellyn Practical Guide to Astral Projection*. Saint Paul, Minnesota, 1979, p.205.

42. Robert Monroe, *Journeys Out of the Body*. Garden City, New York: Doubleday, 1977.

CHAPTER 5:

1. Quoted by Jowett in *The Works of Plato*. New York: Tudor Publishing Company, undated.

2. *Ibid*.

3. *Ibid*.

4. Conan Doyle, *The History of Spiritualism*. New York: George H. Doran Co., 1926, p.280.

5. Plutarch, *Life of Cimon*, translated by John Dryden, in *Plutarch's Lives*. New York and Pittsburgh: The Colonial Company, Ltd., 1905, pp.205-6.

6. *Ibid*, p.199.

7. Pliny the Younger, quoted by Lewes Lavater, *Of Ghostes and Spirites Walking by Nyght*. Reprinted from the 1572 edition by the Oxford University Press, 1929.

8. *The History of Herodotus*, translated by George Rawlingson. New York: John Murray, 1862.

9. George Lyman Kittredge, *Witchcraft in Old and New England*. New York: Russell and Russell, 1958, p.43.

10. Lafcadio Hearn, *Gleanings In Buddha-Fields*. Boston: Houghton, Miflin, & Co., 1897.

11. Martin Ebon, *Reincarnation In the Twentieth Century*. New York: New American Library, 1970, pp.34-5.

12. Morey Bernstein, *The Search For Bridey Murphy*. New York: Avon Books, 1975, pp.173-4.

13. *Ibid*, p.147.

14. *Ibid*, p.182.

15. Eliphas Levi, *The Mysteries of Magic*, translated by Arthur Edward Waite.

London: George Redway, 1886, p.105.

16. Arthur Edward Waite, *The Holy Kabbalah*. New York: University Books, 1972, p.256.

17. Madame H. P. Blavatsky, *Raja Yoga, or Occultism*. Bombay: The Theosophy Company, 1931, pp.92-3.

18. Madame H. P. Blavatsky, *Isis Unveiled*. Los Angeles, California: The Theosophy Company, 1968, vol.1, p.xxx.

19. *Ibid*.

20. Madame H. P. Blavatsky, *Key to Theosophy*. London: The Theosophical Publishing Company, 1889.

21. A. P. Sinnett, *Incidents In the Life of H. P. Blavatsky*. London: George Redway, 1886, pp.177-9.

22. *Ibid*, p.133.

23. *Ibid*, p.179.

CHAPTER 6:

1. Robert Crookall, *Out of the Body Experiences, A Fourth Analysis*. Secausus, New Jersey: The Citadel Press, 1980, pp.74-85. The same thesis is also briefly referred to in Crookall's other books.

2. Ruth Montgomery, *Here and Hereafter*. Greenwich, Connecticut: Fawcett Publications, 1968.

3. F. W. H. Myers, *Human Personality and Its Survival of Bodily Death*. London: Longmans, Green & Co., 1904, vol.2, pp.571-2.

4. Madame H. P. Blavatsky, *Key to Theosophy*. London: The Theosophical Publishing Company, 1889.

5. Lafcadio Hearn, *Gleanings in Buddha-Fields*. Boston: Houghton Miflin and Co., 1897.

CHAPTER 7:

1. Quoted by Madame H. P. Blavatsky, *Isis Unveiled*. Los Angeles, California: The Theosophy Company, 1968, vol.1, p.484.

2. Dr. Maurice Rawlings, *Beyond Death's Door*. New York: Bantam Books, 1979, p.44.

3. *Ibid*, p.45.

4. *Ibid*, pp.45, 47, 85.

5. Karlis Osis, Ph.D., Erlendur Haraldsson, Ph.D., *At the Hour of Death*. New York: Avon Books, 1977.

6. Raymond A. Moody, Jr., *Life After Life*. Atlanta, Georgia: Mockingbird Books, 1976, p.126.

7. Raymond A. Moody, Jr., *Reflections on Life After Life*. Atlanta, Georgia: Mockingbird Books, 1977, pp.45-6.

8. Annie Besant, *The Ancient Wisdom*. London: The Theosophical Publishing Society, 1897.

9. Ithell Colquhoun, *The Sword of Wisdom*. New York: G. P. Putnam's Sons, 1975, p.235.

10. Edgar Allen Poe, *The Premature Burial*, in *The Prose Tales of Edgar Allen Poe*. New York: J. Widdleton, 1878.

11. Emmanuel Swedenborg, *Heaven And Its Wonders, And Hell*, translated by J. C. Ager, New York: The American Swedenborg Printing and Publishing Company, 1925, p.385.

12. *Ibid*, p.380.

13. *Ibid*, p.263.

14. *Ibid*, p.380.

15. *Ibid*, p.381.

16. *Ibid*, p.359.

17. *Ibid*, p.381.

18. *Ibid*, pp.372, 381.

19. *Ibid*, p.380.

20. *Ibid*, pp.263, 382.

21. *Ibid*, pp.263, 75.

22. *Ibid*, p.263.

23. *Ibid*, p.382.

24. *Ibid*, pp.75, 358-359.

25. *Ibid*, p.360.

26. *Ibid*, p.354.

27. *Ibid*, p.355.

28. *Ibid*, p.312.

29. Choegyam Trungpa, *Cutting Through Spiritual Materialism*. Berkeley, California: Shambhala Publications, 1973.

30. Eliphas Levi, *La Clef des Grands Mystères*. Paris: Diffusion Scientifique, updated, pp.110-111.

CHAPTER 8:

1. Sax Rohmer (Arthur Sarsfield Ward), 'Astral Voyages', in *Pall Mall Gazette*, September, 1935.

2. Israel Regardie, *Tree of Life*. New York: Samuel Weiser, 1978.

3. A. P. Sinnett, *The Occult World*. New York: J. W. Bouton, 1884, p.183.

4. Op. cit., p.115.

5. Rama Prasad, *Patanjali's Yoga Sutras*. Allahabad, 1912, p.226.

6. *Ibid*.

7. *Ibid*, also James Houghton Woods, *The Yoga System of Patanjali*. Delhi: Motilal Barnasidass, 1972, p.257.

8. Rama Prasad, op. cit.

Index

By the same author

INVISIBILITY
Mastering the Art of Vanishing

Contains all the theory and practice necessary for using an amazing occult technique! The first book ever to examine this extraordinary subject in depth. Steve Richards (who also wrote *Levitation*), reveals techniques drawn from alchemy, Rosicrucianism, medieval magic, and esoteric yoga, relating them to known scientific phenomena. *Includes:* Producing the electron-cloud (which makes things invisible) in seven steps; A Rosicrucian invisibility recipe; The Invisibility Ritual of the Hermetic Order of the Golden Dawn; Transparency and invisibility; Invisibility by complete absorption; How to do the Harpocrates Assumption.

INVISIBILITY
MASTERING THE ART OF VANISHING

A GUIDE TO HIDING YOURSELF FROM SIGHT USING
TECHNIQUES CULLED FROM ALCHEMY, ROSICRUCIANISM,
MEDIEVAL MAGIC AND ADVANCED YOGIC PRACTICES
Steve Richards

LEVITATION

What it is – How it works – How to do it

Illustrated. Can man fly? This book demonstrates that levitation really is possible, and reveals some practical secrets which could enable *you* to cheat the laws of gravitational force! These secrets are centuries old, hitherto known only to adepts and fakirs. This remarkable book gives you all the relevant facts, the history, the controversies, the theories, and the techniques – everything, in fact, you should know about levitation. A Transcendental Meditation instructor claims that improved mind-body co-ordination can result in levitation – a phenomenon derived from one of the Eight Great Siddhis in yogic tradition.